The Southern Poetry Anthology

Volume II: Mississippi

The Southern Poetry Anthology

Volume II: Mississippi

Edited by

Stephen Gardner and William Wright

Texas Review Press

Huntsville, Texas

FIRST EDITION, 2010
Requests for permission to reproduce material from this work should be sent to:

Permissions
Texas Review Press
English Department
Sam Houston State University
Huntsville, TX 77341-2146

Cover photo: Eudora Welty, LLC; Eudora Welty Collection—Mississippi
      Department of Archives and History
Cover design by Paul Ruffin

Library of Congress Cataloging-in-Publication Data

The Southern poetry anthology. Volume II, Mississippi / [edited by]
Stephen Gardner and William Wright. -- 1st ed.

    p. cm.

  ISBN-13: 978-1-933896-24-3 (pbk. : alk. paper)

  ISBN-10: 1-933896-24-8 (pbk. : alk. paper)

  1. American poetry--Mississippi. I. Gardner, Stephen Leroy, 1948-
II. Wright, William, 1979-

  PS558.M7S67 2010

  811.008'09757--dc22

                                    2010005976

The Southern Poetry Anthology

Volume II: Mississippi

Two down. Thirteen or fourteen to go, depending on how one delineates "South."

We decided that Mississippi would have to be the state on which the second edition of our multi-volume anthology would focus. After all, one of us is here, nestled in the piney woods of Hattiesburg, having just completed his Ph.D. in creative writing at Southern Miss.

Sure, it'd be a breeze. After all, the South Carolina edition only took *years* to complete from start to finish.

But we were optimistic: We'd learned the in-and-outs of editing a considerably large book, all while satisfying the meticulous eyes of almost eighty contributing South Carolinian poets. No easy task.

But Mississippi is different, and this isn't to suggest that South Carolina, or that any other southern state, lacks a substantial literary reputation: Pat Conroy, George Garrett, and James Dickey spring to mind. And we'd like to think that our first volume of *The Southern Poetry Anthology*, centering on our beloved home state, has shown that poets of that area, beginning or experienced, continue to toil in that most difficult and unappreciated of arts: poetry.

Mississippi, though, brims with literary heritage: Eudora Welty, William Faulkner, Barry Hannah, Richard Ford, Larry Brown, Walker Percy, Lewis Nordan, D.C. Berry, T.R. Hummer, Ellen Douglas, Richard Wright, Willie Morris, Elizabeth Spencer. We were treading on intimidating territory, a place where words have been chiseled and reaped and sculpted out of the pine forests and deltas, the muddy creeks and deciduous woodlands, the old families and the old ways continuously decaying and giving way to rich new literary realities. We hope this book, our second volume, adds to that fecundity, and proves that, however long the list or luminous the state's voices, Mississippi's poets deserve their due attention, their chance to shine alone.

There will be people who know that they should be in here but are not. We reached out every way that we knew how: statewide newspapers, mailed calls for manuscripts, notices to societies, word of mouth. We made direct appeals to many poets; some, for reasons known only to themselves, elected not to reply, even to multiple pleadings. As in the South Carolina edition, we regret their absence here, but that choice was theirs. Some contacted us; but, after that contact, they failed to deliver the goods. Some small, rare few were unwilling (or, giving the best thought to the matter, unable) for whatever reason to provide us with necessary information concerning copyright ownership and/or notice of previous publication.

South Carolina and Mississippi down, somewhere else to go.

We gratefully thank the following who, in one way (or in multiple ways) have assisted in bringing this anthology to life:

Chancellor Thomas Hallman and Executive Vice Chancellor for Academic Affairs Suzanne Ozment of the University of South Carolina Aiken, for their support of this project;

The Aiken Partnership and G.L. Toole Chair Endowment, for providing fiscal resources;

Dr. Paul Ruffin and the staff at Texas Review Press, for their willingness to believe and to trust us to bring this volume into being and for being financial partners in the process;

Liz Thompson, Mary Alice Welty White, and the Mississippi Department of Archives and History for the use of the cover photograph;

Our friends and students and loved ones who endured, with grace and understanding, the occasional slight or edginess when the work sometimes turned to burden instead of the normal pleasure;

And the gifted writers included herein, for honoring us with the permission to reproduce their work and present it to you.

William G. Wright, Hattiesburg, MS
Stephen L. Gardner, Aiken, SC

Table of Contents

The Southern Poetry Anthology

Volume II: Mississippi

LESLIE ADAMS

If the Child's Face Is Also a Small House

When we look again, the sun will be gone,
although it will doubtlessly circle back to stand behind us,
discarding shadows at our feet.

And the child, who stands behind us, who makes us seem taller,
will also circle back to stand twelve years behind us,
and call forward words that we are unable to hear at this distance,

and wave frantically in greeting or warning,
and will not be lost in the coming dusk.,
and will not be silenced.

But your face braces itself like the early lines of a house that will not shelter;
I have lived under your jaw for too long
not to recognize the grinding teeth like the sharpening edge of a knife.

I have seen your jaw set like a sun.
I have done this now for many nights, at your feet like a child.

Unlike me, the child is wise, and not easily fooled, or caught.

I do not yet know if the child's face is also a small house,
or whether I would be invited in.

Why should we question this?

The dead are aligned exactly as we left them,
and the unborn still whisk just over our heads, like birds
for whom I half-cast the net and draw it back empty of even air.

Come here, little one.
I will not refuse your questions,
and will not cast nets or accusations.

I dreamed each one of your teeth like unearthed seeds, but here, see,
they have been in my hands all the while.

Wanting the Earth

So this is why imagination, like love, thrives on absence:

the light here won't let us think;
we are ruined by accuracy.

The sea calls back its waves like a falconer,
each morning wakes into place on cue,

heat runs like the hot slap of sap down the ruined trunks of trees,
and the sky, unchanging as an eye, posing water,
drags horizon like the train of a wedding dress;

so studied, everything, so choreographed,

breaking down into other, compressing and reassembling,
sand clamoring back to shale and granite, formless and reforming—

so this is mortality, this is what the word means:
touch and the loss of touch, sight and the failure of sight,

the rain scattering pizzicato, the burden of the stilled string—

Three Graces

1. The Song of Transience

There is nothing of the body that is not innocence,
not the scars and not the flesh between the scars,

not bone with its one straight hard mark;

and not the mind, which is our many fictions,
and is as much our name as any other—

2. Adaptation of Myth into Song

No roots have ever asked their questions of the soil,
and already limbs grow accustomed to new winds.
At the right distance, any name sounds like your own—

It's never a far walk to a place you are unrecognizable,
where it becomes hard for you to pronounce your own name,
where a name becomes the weight you lose and keep losing.

3. The Song of Arbitrariness

And what is the eyelash weight of the first cells,
the weight of the mother who grieves the weight of the child,
the weight of a mind that has forgotten itself?

Let everything spin out as long as it must,
and let the people stumble in their rush to agree with each other,
and in their rush to disagree with each other;

there is no better or worse: there is only other and other,
there is only the building that falls and the building that does not fall,
the hand that grasps and the hand that releases and keeps releasing.

ANGELA BALL

That Was Me

> *I lose myself in others' dreams*
> —John Ashbery

That was me, wasn't it, in your dream, marinating a steak?
Unseen, concocting something astringent, something orange-y,
While whisking hair from my eyes.

Do you know what I look like?
Have I been a sigh joining one dream to the next? Or a companion
On your visit
To an ocean resort?

I'm sure I was in the car
Looking for the turnoff, the suitcase you dropped
And would never go back for.

Night is ample and bossy,
Snatching us this way and that inside its silk steam, its patio
Of drooping palms. My dreams stand at the windows.

Big Colt

It took ten blacksmiths to forge
His shoes; a dozen people at a time

Could pat his forehead.
The big colt stood on the Continental Divide:

One eye saw a carnival; the other, a prison.
When the big colt neighed

There was a landslide.
His birth was difficult. Afterward
His mother shrank to a tiny drawing
On the wall of a cave: chalk

And the blood of berries.

Fence

Late in the day, the wire loses
Its decisiveness, the posts fade
To charcoal strokes
On top of snow. Inside the barn,
Hanging bulbs, the delicate beads
Of their chains, yellowish scrolls
Of flypaper, the warmth
Of horseflesh, manure and piss
Rich and acrid, bridles and saddles
Dangling from their nails—a tang
Of neat's-foot oil, salt, and mossy tobacco.

I mucked the stalls. Now and then
I got by with pushing the stained straw
To the back and covering it
With clean. My sister caught me, asked,
"How would you like
To lie down on dirty straw?

Now I resemble
A horse put to grass,
Eating myself polite inch
By polite inch
Across the indestructible pasture.

Jazz

I'd like to know everything
A jazz artist knows, starting with the song,
"Goodbye Pork Pie Hat."

Like to make some songs myself:
"Goodbye Rickshaw,"
"Goodbye Lemon Drop,"
"Goodbye Rendezvous."

Or maybe even blues:

If you fall in love with me, I'll make you pancakes
All morning. If you fall in love with me
I'll make you pancakes all night.
If you don't like pancakes
We'll go to the creperie. If you don't like pancakes
We'll go to the creperie.
If you don't like to eat, handsome boy,
Don't you hang around with me.

On second thought, I'd rather find
The fanciest music and hear all of it.

I'd rather love somebody
And say his name to myself every day
Until I fall apart.

What to Wear for Divorce

Bats in your hair,
But only if they can hang upside down
Properly.

Putty on your hands,
Butter in your mouth.

Be the feather in someone's cap,
The spyglass in the pirate's hand,
The podiatrist's foot, asleep.

Be the bewildered woman
Half lifting her skirts to cross a muddy street
While a rain cloud watches.

Wear something worn first
By a wolf.

STEVEN BARTHELME

Father

Woods have names:
pine, oak, ash, birch,
redwood, rosewood,
and some you didn't know
or never mentioned
I learned of later—
cordobé and purple heart.

"This is walnut," you'd say,
and in the silence
I heard the heavy-lidded air.

We trusted pine, I guessed,
because it was good and simple wood,
but blond and prone to split;
oak was fine, but Episcopalian wood;
redwood pretty, not beautiful;
mahogany a whore, a rich one;
the only other one you loved
was birch—
almost walnut—
but you didn't say it
with the same faith.

"There's a trick to it," you'd say,
if only you'd come and tell
why the wood and word
provide me no quiet now.

She Cares. Aria Blattaria.

She's tall and her hair
swings to her waist
as she swings the folded newspaper
hard against the poet
running diagonally
up the wall.
"They breed," she says,
"by the thousands."

The glazed brick floor,
she explains, makes it hard
to see them sometimes
with their wineskins
and foreign cheeses
held out front like artillery.
Still, she kills three
while we talk.

It's this way all through
the preparations for dinner
(pasta, tomato sauce, etc).
In the kitchen she uses
an aerosol, in her left hand;
the right never stops stirring.
Pzzzzzzz. "Damned poets," she says,
"and their Orioles—
sick birds and sand."

She wondered, she tells me
while we eat,
why the place was so cheap.

Late in the evening
she checks the motels.

"Sometimes," she says,
staring into one brown box,
"you get a pregnant one,
with all these little poets
stuck behind like BBs,
talking about Volkswagens

or brand name trees.
Yak yak yak yak.
Until they dry up."

We adjourn.
The sheets immaculate
like typing paper,
her skin soft,
her voice like several
different rains.

I don't say so.

I say,
"I had a place once
so infested
they skipped across ice cubes
in the freezer, and
a man with one hand came
with a fogging machine,
the compressor so loud
the cat jumped off the balcony.
For two years after,
no poets."

The glorious hair
spreads under her
falling on two sides over
the edges, down to the brick,
as she lies, saying,
"None? Not one?"

MIKE BASSETT

The Blackboard of His Eyelid

He's a Chihuahua-eyed chicken boy
with hundreds of freckles
his mother swears are seeds
from the pumpkin they carved
him out of. But he knows where
babies come from. He knows the darkness
of the closet, where he listens
to his mother's crying. He learns, under
the henhouse, the weasel's way.

If he had Becky Wilson here,
he'd make her confess that she had lied
about how his parents make him drink
from the toilet and sleep
in a rabbit cage. A pale and skinny
clump of literature, always out past
the curfew of acceptance, behind
enemy lines of imagination, he plays
torturer of the inquisition,
brandishing the garden shears.

On the playground, while he practices
impossible contortions
of introspection, they bloody his nose,
hating the secrets hidden
in the scriptorium of his oddness.
They crack his sharp ribs, desperate
for the futures he reads
on the blackboard of his eyelid.
They shake from his green satchel

two dung beetles, most of a Mabel
Garden Spider, a scab from his skinned
knee, a sliver of bailing wire,
a cat's eye marble, and a quart
of Quick Start lighter fluid.

He can't stop thinking about apricots
shriveling, paint belching, tiny frogs
dripping above matches. Outside his secret
fort, sycamores yellow and cackle.

Clairvoyant

We had to guess at the contents
of the bag she carried. Perhaps
shrouded in tissue the shrunken head
of the chess-playing lobster boy,
a ram's brooding tongue that told the hour
of your death, a five-pointed amulet
trapping women who smiled too much.

We knew the old woman had been a carnival
fortuneteller. She'd squeeze my elbow too hard
turning my small palm over. Children must
be shielded, she said, from the gaze of the Hollow Man.

I worried she knew about the drawings
in the shoe box under my bed
and what we did to Barbie in the shallow
pit out behind the Thompson place.
When I dream of her it is in a city
where all the windows have cataracts.

Cassandra Syndrome

Heaven was on fire. The sky smoked
with a Pete's Cola advertisement.
My grandfather, a boy who had never seen
a car, much less a crop duster
converted into a skywriter, didn't wait
to read the rest of the message. He'd heard
Reverend Quick preach many times on how
the world would PERISH in a wrath of fire.
So he took off like a hunted squirrel.
With his britches still unzipped,
he ran the three miles from Izora Brown
and her daddy's woodpile
to his own family's farmhouse,
where he couldn't get anyone to look.
His mama, mending a quilting loom, told him
to quit such foolishness. And older sister
Jessie said she would maybe come see later,
after the floors were swept.
No one believed his warning.
No one could see the writing
for the wall.

Light & Heavy

I do not know which is worse,
being a memory so hulking fat
your spindly bones are about to snap,
or an unstrung ghost puppet
with wild guesses for a backbone,
insecurity for a left shoe.

While blue siren lights played
over the abandoned tricycle next door,
the police talked to the man, whose
liver-spotted hands triangular
as fish heads shook so badly
he could hardly hold his cigarette.
I had heard the accusations, the shattering
plates of rage. I wondered if it was over
a VISA bill, some other lover, or was it just
the way people find each other by drawing blood.

"He lives alone. Poor crazy bastard.
Wife died years ago," a neighbor told me
while the dryers spun our double loads.

Us and Them

Her hair on my pillow is the peace I'd get as a kid coming in from the ocean to the snoring air conditioning and the smells of coconut and perch cooking. I want to write a poem for the tenderness I feel for her knee socks but instead I dream a solitary kestrel turns into a pale winter sun and finally into my father's face bearded in foam and steam. No matter how I keep his head submerged under my beet-colored resentment, I'll always be in his study full of books too difficult for me. The past should be more pliant. I hope here in this bed she and I are parent-less, not caring about the legacies that crawl like Escher lizards along a Möbius. But she may be lost in pills fetched for her mother. She may be dreaming of her daddy's flannel shirts and her opening bedroom door, the wand of light that doesn't reach.

D.C. BERRY

Skull Lunch Pail

I loathe this play much as I loathe myself:
black clothes, the graveyard shift, the skull lunch-pail.
Nobody's who he is. Who acts like Who.
God's blood. The play's a toilet of questions.
Flush one, another splashes in your face.
The play's first two words shout, "Who's there?"
Good Dr. Freud? What ho? Good Dr. Fraud?
Or Who? I'm psychiatric bait without a hook.
Some nights can't catch a ride after the play.
Me with my empty skull lunch pail. Taxis
just tap the brakes and stare like full hearses:
Sorry, you don't look dead enough, call at midnight.
I yell, "Help your local ventriloquists" and flash
the skull. They squeal off like they think the skull
is the ventriloquist and I—Hambo—the doll.

Hambo Rambo

I ought to be at World Wrestling College,
tackling the craft of Vengeance Theatrics,
honing my Elvis snarls and Hitler sulks,
at least learning to cheat at solitaire.
But can't. Too mother-fuddled. Mom's a cow,
a sex freaknoid, a forked trap door—where's mom?
I've heard her *Moo*. Why do moms keep humping?
Squeeze out a kid, I say, then kiss goodbye
the bedroom coos and sorority war whoops.
I'm born. What but the grunt in mom craves more
mounting? By Claudius? By Claud His Balls.
Kill him, I Hambo shall. I Hambeau Sissy shall
with Hambaud's poems fright him to death: Hamboo!
Hambone him till he gags his soup. Except,
Hollywood waits, wants me to play Hamlet.
Go? Or coax Claude to Gulfport for roulette?
The arrow click on his number, I'll know
the UFO was dad, no devil blowing smoke,
Claude bull, I matador, will prick his soul
till by his weight he splashes on my sword.
His blood will be the cape by which I trump
him, which should chill mother's love of the hump.

Blonde Dittos

I fall in love with two blonds in tight jeans
ahead of me. I catch up and they are—
yank my greasy toupee—they are the girls:
Ophelia and Gertrude, my black-root blondes,
Oh Puke Me and Mon Mom, the Barbie babes.
The two so one, one's ribs the other's harp,
and Claude busy plucking the strings of both.
I won't touch Oh. I'm into deep hygiene.
I'm clean of the whole Maybelline coven.
This boy pounds his baton like Beethoven.

Mel Gibson's Movie of Me

Mel Gibson's *Hamlet*, that's doll Mel. Wind up
Mel, and Mel's eyes melt into bluebird milk,
blue pools of earnestness, and blue Gertrude
sucks it all up, swills Mel's sincerity—
the jokeless Mel, Mel Duh, Mel Doll. Mel knows
a joke's loose only when cued by the laugh
track, Gertrude in his lap, slapping her knee,
making me want to screech my do-die speech
about the dew: dissolve into *adieu*—
adieu, a dew, a do-die dodo you.
The closest dad ever came to a dew
was when, pell mell into the flames, he yelled
adieu/ a dew—a joke lost on doll Mel,
Mel outplayed by even ye olde castle.

Pansy Icelandia and Panty Toast

We're on the coast—Spring Break—bronzing our buffs,
toning Budweiser abs, and our butt-string
yummies sun-tanning their yoyos. But what?
Icelandic cold, ice-cube eyes, I'm depressed.
I got the blues, the pansies got the blues,
bleached in their shiny strait-jackets of frost.
No quandary to our hiney-thonged Gertrude,
out baking panty toast with jet-ski bums,
her buns burning and freezing hot, cold, hot,
in this do-or-die world in which you bid
a grave and call a wedding. Life's a piece
of cake, but wedding cakes are sugared urns.
Give me pansies and their frozen faces.
They wear death as cool as Claudius slides
a wedding band on his dead brother's bride.

TONY BLAND

Driving All Night

He lies in the bed of a foreign
pickup truck, riding across
the desert. It's late, after midnight.

His teenage daughter is driving—
their first all night trip together
since she got her license. He can't sleep.
He knows something is going
to happen: the sudden explosion
of a blowout; a drunken trucker drifting
across the center line; the stupid armadillo
she swerves to avoid. He feels
the constant vibration of
faulty tires and tells himself
he should have had them
balanced before they left home.

He has not been a good father.
He should have talked more, listened
more, spent more time with her
after the divorce. He fidgets
with the pillow, stares up
at the acrylic camper top
between him and the stars.
He wonders if he ever did anything right.

Her eyes follow the headlight beams
racing on into the night. Mile after mile
of desert disappear behind them. Her head moves
to the rhythm of her own music; her hand
rests steady on the wheel.

Nutgrass in the Garden

My mother said many times before
she died, "The only way to get rid
of nutgrass is to move off and leave it."
Now she has moved off and left it. It

no longer invades her garden, but
we must still work ours. My father,
too weak to hoe, sinks to his knees
in the damp earth, small spade

in hand. Something we will never
name is growing inside his body, breaking
it down, cell by cell. Sprig after sprig
he digs it up, knowing all the while that

his efforts are futile. Somewhere
below lie irremovable roots, intertwined
with the earth itself, that keep pushing
the stems up into the light. Still

he digs, making a small haven
around his cucumbers and tomatoes,
not quite yet ready to relinquish
this small piece of ground.

RICHARD BOADA

Double-Birth

Improbably, two foals clumsily approach
their mare. Thin phalanxes and coffin bones
buckle as hoofs slip in the morning grass.
They trust hock joints, pick up gallop,
one snout knocks the other snout. Breaths fog
the air. The mare's a quay in bluegrass
panicles and her young are muscular
vessels that fleck moisture off their black
pelage. They'll run this birth coat off.

Avocet Coup

Refugees, second wives, and cowled
monks squeeze through blear
tourists. A corpse floats

on the surface of the Seine. Water chops
and gulps, pounds the scorched
breasts and face. Birds swarm

over. Fledged men on bridges try to snag
the body out of the water with hooking
ash-poles and nets. Timbery sirens call

all to notice. Police arrive with shotguns.
They fire at the chalky sky; abate
the birds from devouring.

Sunspots

On the last night uncle slept in the country
house that he helped the bank foreclose
from the Alexanders, he didn't say much
before he died, just God's will for the boys
to come back home.

The boys canvassed his acres and took potatoes
and broccoli. They bound his farmhands with rope
and left them huddled in the fields, sucking air
through broken mouths, socked with their own tools:
shovels and hoes, empty whiskey bottles and rifle butts.
The polished oak ends stained red. The boys showed
mercy not to shoot but took the rabbits that hung low
from the sycamore branches near the house instead.

Uncle recognized the boys that held his rabbits, just killed,
still draining blood, over his bed. He saw their daddy's eyes
in each of the boys—freckled grays.

Dye

Naked under chrome faucet penciling
lukewarm water, her face in the convex
drain stop, allelic reflections, cheeks, eyes and nose
indistinct but separate. Those, she'll pass
to her unborn daughters. Hands, a new basin,
bring water to mouth.

With right thumb and forefinger he pulls
the left glove's rubber wristband and releases
it to smack skin. He ties her hair back loose
with ribbon. Smoothes dark-brown deep
onto scalp. Its paleness shocked. She tells him
to pull the hair back harder. Plastic taut on fingernails
he rakes her skull. The ribbon flitting to floor, he dyes.
Gloves greased in permanent brown.

LOUIS E. BOURGEOIS

Overlooking Sardis Reservoir in the Middle of Winter

January afternoon. I look out across the barren lake.
Oaks and pines form the skyline.
A few cedars stand alone in the distance.
Small bayous flow in zigzag fashion through the plain,
and as the sun goes down, hills diminish in the soft evening light.
Ducks and geese crowd the sky with their late migrations,
and buzzards circle and begin to fill the empty trees.

DEVON BRENNER

Secondhand Boots

The night we met I approached him,
talking with his circle about book readings and faculty positions.
I shared from his back-pocket flask of rye poured over
cubes I carried with my bare hands.
Later in the kitchen he showed me his cowboy boots
faded black, elephant hide, secondhand.
We spoke of children and custody,
empty talk about the years I've lived in the South,
the benefits of a meatless diet, language accidents in foreign lands.
The while, I thought of clichés—
the zing when our eyes met,
Cupid's arrow,
love at first sight.
But I walked away,
left him standing under the carport,
ice melting in the bottom of a plastic cup.

Now I wonder if we could get away, steal a weekend in the Delta,
an afternoon on a blanket in a field,
Hell, an encounter in the back seat of a rented car,
halfway between here and there.

It wouldn't be enough, though.
I want to find out the names of his dogs, the music on his shelves,
I want time to clarify the thing I said about going through men like
facial tissue,
to show him the path in the woods west of the cotton fields,
to ask the title of that book he read, forget, and ask again.
I want to learn if we laugh standing in line at airport security,
or waiting our turn at the bakery,

if he likes my minestrone,
which sections of the paper he leaves unread.

I know there are more clichés,
a nearly ex-wife somewhere in California,
a girlfriend in Texas, finishing an M.F.A.,
a job, waiting in Wyoming.

All of it too familiar, like those boots.
All of it just worn out.

JACK BUTLER

No News at All

The weather isn't news unless extreme,
though the news is a kind of grumbling weather—
fortunately far-off and dwindled, tinny,
as voices remembered from a dream.
Men need freshness most. What can offer any?
Not memory and history together.

Only what's outside skin or brain
can make a difference to what's caught in it.
That difference might be nothing more than light,
the rusty odor of dust freckling with rain,
or the rain-drops, dust-floured, dusty white,
that roll about like mercury a minute.

Wild Orders

Let me look on nothing like myself—
let me look on wild orders.
There are always wars at the borders.
There are always borders.

What keeps plant from animal but a name
hidden somewhere inside?
What keeps saint from murderer but a refusal
to accept the blame?

—I came as close as any came.

Oh tongue of seeded flame,
oh visitant of the rank and tattered petals,
let me be butterfly, or blank
as the heart of a star, heart of water:
Come battering
the gates apart, lord hawk, lord frog, lord thing—
but teach me how to sing.

The Changing of Vision with Time

I

My father's hair was black, blue-black back then.
He was a pilot who had flown his plane
into the ground and lived. But war was over,
over forever, and he was home. My mother,
she could have been a movie star,
so pretty and her loose red hair.
The Mississippi was the biggest river,
and I would fly a rocketship in outer space.
I remember when I had a boy's face.

II

Uncles, oh I had aunts and uncles. Dozens.
And Barbara and Wayne were my first cousins.
The land was Butler land, and we stood tall.
My grandfather could do anything at all,
could fix a tractor, build a church,
run a plantation. The front porch
was better than a downtown movie hall,
and the greatest song of all was clearly "Amazing Grace."
I remember when I had a boy's face.

III

Red and blue cellophane, and Captain 3-D
would jump the panels to reality
to save us from the cat-people. If you were true,
if you were honest, God would look after you.
Maybe not with money, but with
good love, good food, good times, good health.
Not even the greatest painter could outdo
the smoky broken violet of the sun's last rays.
I remember when I had a boy's face.

IV

Mornings I left my footprints, oh I left
bright wreckage in the dew-drenched clover-drift,
went in to breakfast. Black men called me Mister
and stepped aside and tipped their hats to my sister
because they knew our family kept
the land together. And when I slept,
I always dreamed of flying, and flying faster,
and later I dreamed of sex, and later I dreamed of grace.
I remember when I had a boy's face.

Paradise Is a Hard Gig

                                    So often
The meanest people live in the finest places.
No chaos of laughter is ever permitted to soften

the bitter disappointment of their faces,
yet nothing is lacking. Everything is full.
Hand after hand they turn up kings and aces

then fold before the pay-off. Their bells toll
a dull salvation to the blessed air,
and dull against their eardrums beat, and roll

in thunderous echoes down their everywhere
green valleys, through which their rivers, fat with trout,
do leap and sparkle. Oh yay dey do, *mon frere,*

Br'er Rabbit. And you know why? Without a doubt
because they are so small against it, because
they take themselves so serious. They shut out

the mornings' breezes, tune their radios
to squawking lowland frequencies, and, grim
with satisfaction, choose the damnedest news

to rebroadcast. No trickster gods for them,
Br'er Fox, Coyote, Crow. And no unbidden
rock-and-roll backbeat to make the black blues scram.

Why, what would it mean if everything were given,
if we were not our own, but children of joy,
that joy which only makes, and only makes heaven?

How would we get our gold stars then, Big Boy?
Affix those medals same color as our bruises?
Spring for the hundred-thousand-dollar toy?

We'd waste our time with double rainbows, roses
in opalescent vases, water-fountains
and apricots and bulldogs and plastic noses

with waggling Groucho mustaches, wild mountains
at mutinous altitudes outside the studio
of ten blue windows, in which we paint our paintings

when we aren't arguing Zen, or watching the snow
come flying in from nowhere like subatomics
at quantum zero, or teaching our wings to grow

from the fourth chakra, or reading the Sunday comics
in bed, or fucking before we read the comics.

The Constancy of Existence

I swore to love forever, why not?
It felt like forever when I saw that languid head sway
on her tall neck. Her eyes were green, sea-green. Grey.
Twenty years ago we split.
Thirty-one years ago we said our vows aloud.
The traveling shadow of a cloud
over uneven mountains.

Children, I had children. I
was a god to them, laughter and thunder and safety.
Now I'm a clown. Beloved of course, but half past fifty.
Our daughters are women now, they cry
at sad movies and rule the world. I tell you, they make me proud.
The traveling shadow of a cloud
over uneven mountains.

I thought of reputation once
for a couple of decades. I had one for a while,
sort of, almost. Now I've developed this steady style
amid the vicissitudes of chance
I hope somebody takes for wisdom, marble-browed.
The traveling shadow of a cloud
over uneven mountains.

He sat in his own shit and wept,
that stinky fellow with a familiar face.
Crippled, infected, pus-ridden, and hideous in disgrace.
His dreams accused him when he slept.
The prisoner of self, no visitors allowed.
The traveling shadow of a cloud
over uneven mountains.

He was a sungod, and he drove
a golden thunderjet across their skies.
He walked among them and they fainted at his eyes:
Such thought, such clarity, such love.
I'm just a simple citizen, he told the crowd.
The traveling shadow of a cloud
over uneven mountains.

Where does life come from? Where does it go?
But what else is there? Why are we haunted by existence,
and why does beauty always disappear to distance?
We practice but we never know.
I wear my happiness like John Donne wore his shroud.
The traveling shadow of a cloud
over uneven mountains.

My lover is aging like a creek
in yellow aspen. That season, that altitude.
I think of palomino horses when I see her nude.
Sometimes we laugh too hard to speak.
Come see, I called, *come quick.* And we oohed and aahed and wowed:
The traveling shadow of a cloud
over uneven mountains.

FRED CLARKE

The Meaning of the Apples

I.

See the woman
suspended on a highway,
on the lips of the ocean.
One determined step into the wind
would pull her under with a sigh
and the other
would accept head-on the predetermined end:

A piece of driftwood
And the green lights that bubbled
In its wake.

II.

Remembers
a backyard,
rose bushes on the fence, rusted
swing set under apple trees.
heat-lightning on the horizon, mingling
with the smell of lilac and moss.

She bent
the branches and
put the apples in a wagon.
Small, green, bitter.

III.

No trees, no apples
rotting in a backyard. Only stumps:
no one to know
the meaning of the apples.

The Existence of Memory

The existence of forgetting has never been proved:
we only know that some things do not come to mind
when we want them. —Nietzsche

First she forgot simple things:
points of a conversation, words

here and there, the handbag in her hands.
She spent an hour looking for that bag

before she found where she left it,
misplaced on her person, laughing, chalking it up to—

something, she forgot what. Something to do
with the absence of color in her hair,

the presence of lines around her eyes. She was somewhere
between wanting and incapable

to get in the car and drive to the hospital.
Once there, next to him, she couldn't recall

her hands on the wheel, her face in the rearview,
but she was there in time to spend

the last moments, bent
over his head. She didn't remember the face

later, standing in the window, looking
to see his eyes in her reflection,

searching for resolution, not finding
answers. She wiped tears with the napkin in her hand,

hid the napkin neatly in her handbag.

metaphor one

i gave a poem
to my 6th grade
teacher to read

she told me to
dig deeper

is that a
metaphor
i asked
she asked
what
do you think

i asked her
for a shovel

BETH COUTURE

Three on Dragonflies

Dream

A girl dreams she eats a dragonfly. She pulls it from high in the air above her head, pinches it between her thumb and forefinger, and brings it to her lips, encases it behind straight white teeth. It buzzes angrily, its wings beating against the roof of her mouth. She is lucky it is a dream. It would destroy her if it could, would tear her apart with fierce mandibles, dig its way down her throat and into her heart. The girl who eats the dragonfly doesn't chew but swallows it whole, feels it take flight within her belly. When she wakes, the air surrounding her is full and loud, thick with the humming of wings. She looks up, stretches an arm over her head and snatches one of the cobalt insects from the air. It cannot buzz, and jerks—trying to remove itself from the tissue-thin membranes attached to its back. She holds it, staring at its legs turning over each other. If they could kick, they would bruise. Instead she watches as they scrabble, helpless and dangling. She brings it to her mouth and this time, she bites down.

The Horse Stinger

When she was six, her older brother made her a toy out of grasses and twigs. At first, it looked like a ladybug, and then a bumblebee. Finally, it became a Horse Stinger with grass for its body and twigs for its legs, and wings made from large shiny leaves. Short, stiff grasses made antennae, and he placed tiny glossy rocks on its head for eyes. He told her it would protect her from anyone who tried to harm her. "Look," he said, "he has sharp teeth and strong jaws, and he can bite anything that scares you. Nothing will come near you while you have him." At first she was scared of her toy. She was scared of its round,

shining eyes, of the wings that hung from its segmented back. She was afraid of its teeth, its jaws that looked ready to bite down on anything that got near them. Most of all, she was afraid of the needle-like tail that grew out of its backside, its sharp silvery point that reflected sunlight. But each day she brought the Horse Stinger outside with the rest of her toys and played with them until sunset, and nothing ever harmed her. She didn't know if this was because of the Horse Stinger, but she became less and less afraid of the toy as the summer days wore on.

One day she was playing in the sunshine when a man in a dark suit came and sat down next to her under the oak tree. He smiled at her, but she saw that his teeth were yellowed and sharp like a cat's. "Can I play with you?" he asked, reaching for the Horse Stinger. She didn't know what happened, but she heard a buzzing and the man pulled his hand back like it had been burned, like he had touched a hot stove or a porcupine. She looked at the Horse Stinger and saw its wings beginning to move and its jaws working furiously. It snapped at the man's hand, drew blood, and raised itself off the ground by beating its wings. "You'd better run," she said to the man, and he looked scared, but so scared he didn't move. He was stuck in concrete or made of wood, he was so still, but the Horse Stinger was not still and moved toward him before he could even scream. When it was done with him, there was blood covering the ground under the oak tree. When it was done with him, he could no longer see, or speak, or feel. The Horse Stinger had bound his eyes, his mouth, his fingers with silver thread, and the man just lay under the oak tree like a sad sightless worm.

Lies

My grandmother used to tell me if I ever told a lie they would come to me at night and sew my lips together. She said dragonflies know if children lie, the Devil tells them, and they fly in your window at night while you're asleep and sew up your mouth so you can never lie again. I tried it one day, and told her I got an A on my English homework when really I had only gotten an A minus. Not a big lie, but Grandmother had said any lie would do. That night I lay in bed, not sleeping, the covers pulled up over my mouth just in case. In the morning when I woke up and could still talk, I told my grandmother what I had done, that the dragonflies hadn't come. She said not to be too sure they wouldn't; they would come when I didn't expect them to. "The Devil never forgets," she said.

And so when I woke up one night and saw Grandmother standing over my bed with her needle and her spool of thick black thread, when she put her finger to my lips and told me not to say a word, I knew. She had tied my arms and legs to the bed, tightly, soundlessly. She bit off a yard of thread, poked it through the eye of the needle, and began her work. By the time I thought to scream, the needle had pierced my lips, had pulled the thread through the bottom lip, then the top, and I could only whimper. My grandmother worked silently, just like all the nights when she sat by the fire darning socks, my dresses, Grandfather's work pants. She worked silently, and the only sounds I heard were the thread being pulled taut through my lips and the rustling of her wings.

λ

JACK CROCKER

The Older You Get the More You Appreciate Heat

It kicked off
Sometime Saturday night
Surprising the hell out of us
And October
Hushing up everything so
I swear you could hear a roach spit.

Lord, the world was white.

I told the wife
We'll have to turn up the heat
And put on the soup
For it was colder
As the man says
Than a polar bear's ass.

She said come look
The fence posts are like candles
Stuck in a birthday cake

And I said get on back to bed
And warm me woman
This ain't no time for poetry.

The Last Resort

You conquer loss by going to the place it happened,
                                        Hugo said,
A thought to hang on when all else fails,

Which is to say I can always go back to the
Contented farm and fat sunrise.
                                        The old house
Will take me in like a seed and I will wax whole
Again in a field of memories unkillable as weeds:
                                        My father's
Morning whistle wavering through the tractor's cough;
                                        My mother's
Motherly shriek at the chalk snake I coiled beneath my
Pillow;
                                        The barefoot
Hope that turned the yard green with jonquils every spring. . .

Back and forth back and forth I worry the old ruts like
A furrowing plow until I get to the bare
                                        Bones of grief.

I have forgotten the date my mother died.
                                        The day was hot.
I have forgotten the date my father died.
                                        The day was cold.
I have never laid the simple grief of flowers on their graves,
                                        The granite inventory
Of nothing left but chiseled names, dates, and a few
                                        Cold words.

What could I take there to the sunned slopes and patient grass
That I couldn't give here now where the narcissus I planted
                                        On my little plot
Of ground brings back spring and the words of a poem
                                        To lean on?

Lifting Weights

It starts with getting up in the morning,
The muscles pullying against the brain's dark
Opposition, feet swinging to the floor,
Lifting the body upright, the vertical
Affirmation of accepting another day.

The barbell lies in wait, heavy rings
Of history stacked on each end.
Will there be an add-on today?
How much will it weigh?

The twenty pounders are constant, with dates:
Birth, marriage, holy days;
Side by side with leaden absences:
Deaths, divorce, love's broken anchor.

Added to these are the right words
Never spoken and the little ten-pound
Memories of unintended brutalities
And habitual deceptions that fatten guilt.

Small, mundane, flat tire moments
Leap on with temporary weight.

And then there is the Idea of God the Spotter
That won't go away even though He is not here,
All the contradictions having led to His dead weight,
Changing the sanguine burden of being
To the plumbic press of being alone.

What the head dreads the heart takes on
Until at night, horizontal again, the laden
I presses on the chest, and just before sleep
The thought comes of how little ashes weigh.

GEORGE DREW

The Woman the Blues Are About

She is not afraid of purple,
lavender, and various shades of blue,
likes Mississippi John Hurt
better than Eric Clapton,
and absolutely adores Bessie and Billie,
Ella, and Koko Taylor, too.

She likes music of all kinds,
and likes the downward rush and tumble
of mountain brooks in spring,
likes the raucous off-key kinetics
of the world she thunders through.

She is not afraid of angry men
who are deep down cowards
and violent because they are cowards,

and when she finds the man
who gives her flowers when she frowns
and gives her camels
when distance weighs her down,

she will shoulder him and her guitar
and ride the rails on out of town.

The World after Mama

1927-2007
For my brother

1: Ain't That Something

This ain't the Delta but the morning
after Mama died the land is lush
with corn ready for the picking
and tomatoes plump as dumplings
on the vine and squash and peas,
and though the Hudson River ain't
the Big Muddy, looking down on it
as I am, I'd like to say it's brown
as her big eyes, but that would be a lie.
The truth is otherwise. The Hudson's blue,
and with the sunrise flaring like
ripe watermelon in the west all
I can say is, the only thing near
as lovely as the day Mama was born
is the day she became a permanent part
of nothing. Now ain't that something.

2: One Hour Till Touchdown (In Memphis)

Maybe if I wish it hard enough
it will still be 1953 and Elvis
and my cousin Bobby will be
sitting together on a curb and Elvis
will be playing his cheap guitar
and all the guys and gals will
gather round to listen to the King
before he was the King wailing away,
and maybe by the time we touch down
Mama won't be dead and she'll
be waiting at the baggage carousel
and when she sees me smile
that big smile of hers, and maybe yes,
Elvis himself will pick us up in his
gold Cadillac, and Mama on my arm
we'll cruise Beale, every joint jumping.

3: A Pot of Black-Eyed Peas

The doctors said Mama was gone
before she hit the floor and suffered
the gash that went from her mouth
to her chin, and when he saw her body
my brother Gerald Raymond couldn't
help but wonder what her last
thought was in that last split
second on the last day of her life.
Did she think of her sister Joyce
beside whose bed she was keeping
watch when her heart gave out?
Was it of her long departed daddy,
of all the things she never got to say?
A pot of black-eyed peas bubbling away?
Or was she thinking Closer my God to Thee,
and hoping it was so, hoping it was so?

4: It Didn't Look Like Mama

Everybody said it didn't look like Mama.
Her hair wasn't right for one thing,
and oh good lord her mouth:
closed tight, it suffocated the big smile
she met Gerald Raymond and his wife Jan
with each Saturday when they came to visit.
It took me an hour to work up nerve
enough to walk up to the casket and see
for myself, but when I finally did I saw
it was Mama all right—those hands,
that solid chin, those high cheekbones,
that crop of liver spots—but Mama
altered by death and the mortician's craft.
As for her mouth what did they know?
If I kissed her, her lips would be icy cold,
but cold or hot, smiling or not, Mama.

5: Calling on Peter

The hole they lowered Mama into was
in the section of the cemetery nearest
the row of cedars and white pines.
From them the birds sang harmony
to the locusts that were so numerous
they damn near drowned out the prayer
the preacher led us in, its final lines
calling on Peter to open the pearly gates
to the dear departed soul of Willie Sue.
Sweat glistened in the Delta heat
and after the service, voices thick
as Mama's biscuits, everyone professed
eternal gratitude for the shade the trees
provided, and from the field on the other
side shining through the branches acres
and acres of little cotton balls of light.

6: Waiting for Jan to Pick Me Up

Today, six days after Mama died
and two after she was lowered into
earth, the emails in my box are junk
and after only five of the thirty minutes
I'm allowed online I'm outside just
down the street from the library
waiting for Jan to pick me up. Standing
before the County Courthouse, I inspect
the decrepit building directly opposite,
at 69 Delta Street: it's gray brick, has
a Depression-era red tin roof, and ivy
strangling all the edges and both sides.
It's a cool day, gray, with steady rain
and the old brick building's nearly done,
but today the world after Mama begins
and here comes Jan. Bring it on.

Possum

Gus grinned. "Watch this," he said,
and walked up to the possum where
it lay beneath the cypress playing dead.
Once. . . twice. . . three times he slammed the butt
of his shotgun against the possum's skull.
The possum pissed. "Now watch," Gus said.
He turned his back to the possum,
then walked away. Nine paces…ten,
and up the possum hopped and off
it waddled straight into the swamp.
Gus turned and shot the possum dead.

The echo rolled across the swamp. "You see,"
Gus said, "the critter has a head
as hard as daddy's liquor used to be."
The possum twitched. Gus grinned.
Again he raised his shotgun high
and brought the butt down hard against
the possum's head. The head erupted blood.
"Goddamn antiques!" Gus spat. *I know*, I said.

The End of Lonely Street

The camera pans sadly over the double
bed across the room, and the point is made:
he's young, in love, alone, and singing the blues,
oh since my baby left me, his yellow hair cascading
over his blue eyes. *You make me so lonely baby*,
he moans, which means: Old Buddy, I ain't
gonna get none tonight, which means:
an empty heart is Purgatory but an empty bed
is Hell. The camera cuts, closing in on his face,
the lighting dimmed to a dusty glow
that gathers to a blackness as he tells the tale
he has to tell in lyrics more lachrymose than
the bell hop's tears on what is shaping up
to be a rainy night *down at the end of Lonely Street*
somewhere in Nowhere, USA, which means:
the desk clerk's still dressed in black, the cost
hasn't changed, and the tale is an old one.
But the hotel where he's *found a new place to dwell*
is a motel, the motel's chic not seedy, and damn it,
he's sure as hell not going to die—not this broken
hearted lover, and not, *not*, in this motel.

KENDALL DUNKELBERG

Ishtar

In Kurnugi, the land
of the dead, men
grow feathers, eat
clay for bread, drink
dust, wait for spring,
wait for Ishtar
to shed each jewel,
even the garnet
of her own body.

Mississippi is like this,
a scorched dark country
where silence solidifies
like clay in a kiln. Time
glazes and cracks over
the cool black obsidian
of a crow, so dark
he glistens blue-green
to purple at the neck.

Rubies burn in
place of eyes, as I
spread my wings, ruffle
my emerald necklace,
open my gold encrusted
beak in an inaudible caw.

I tell myths, some
would call them rumors,
some memories. Others
whisper they are nothing

more than the desire to see
your silver bracelets fall,
to feel your cool breath ruffle
the feathers on my spine.

If you will enter
this nether world,
I will gather you
in soft plumage,
clothe your body
in silence. Together
we will drink water.
We will both revive.

Glass Bottles

Lying next to you, I begin to remember
all the words I ever stored in bottles,
to unearth from dream and memory
the stories that wrote me down the way
you found me. Their blue-green, whorled
glass is resurrected from the earth, much
like the bottles my cousins used to dig up
in the woods around Crete, Illinois.

Some were cracked and broken; some
were whole, but caked with soil
that had to be brushed off carefully
to reveal each brand's own distinctive
shape and color. Then they rinsed out
the insides and polished until each one
sparkled. Some were worth no more
than the original nickel deposit,
but the rare, old, odd-shaped ones
that once held hair tonic or snake oil,
these could be worth a fortune.

In her cellar, my Grandma kept magic
green Ball and blue Mason jars filled
with home preserves. It was the coolest,
darkest corner closet of the basement
where she also kept depression ware
and where my Grandpa would stand
beneath a cool white fluorescent light
and play us jigs and reels on his fiddle.

I want to pour out these stories slowly
for you, as if anointing your body
with sandalwood or myrrh. I want to
mingle my past with yours and blow
new glass vessels, wild and ornate ones,
where we can store our own words,
the ones we say together.

Chivaree

after The Horn Island Logs of Walter Ingliss Anderson

He comes here to flee madness
and obligations on shore
yet the human world
can never completely be
lost or left behind.

The military high road,
devoid of vegetation,
makes a good pathway
when he is not progressing
through swamps and lagoons.

Rabbit Springs provides water
from a well the army dug.
It's his only source
until he sinks an old tin
can into the sand.

Even the mosquitoes are
easier to bear with *Flit*
and the biting ants
can be driven far away
with its toxic spray.

He watches ships and barges
pass daily through the channel.
A banana boat
loses its cargo and feeds
the island for weeks.

In the night, drunken hunters
come to give a chivaree,
pounding on his boat
as a reminder of wife
and children at home.

Farm on a Hill

Oh, if I could paint
this hill in a poem,
the way the meadow
sweeps down, pale green
grass and a few junipers
the only signs of life now.
Copses of bare trees
fill the curves of the S
and on top, stands
an abandoned farmhouse,
white, peeling to gray,
windswept and forlorn,
but oh, the perseverance
of those farmers once,
proud, nearly foolhardy
to build their home
where they could
survey their domain.
Safe from floods, yes,
but battered by winter winds
as if defying the elements
that laugh around it now.
Though it wasn't the wind
that drove the farmer out,
but the volatile price
of corn and the promise
of an easier life in town.

DEJA EARLEY

Muddy Waters and the Cat

The dapper Muddy Waters paces
the porch, waiting for his woman.

When the eyes he catches are crossed,
he drops his hat. The crosseyed cat

stares him down, purring. Muddy steps,
stomps to scare it out of its glare,

but the cat just pauses, unfazed,
licks a paw. He freezes mid-lick

to give another crooked look.
Muddy shakes his head.

Reminds himself the woman looks good.
He's here because the woman looks good.

Bowl

When I draw a bath, my cat thinks
I am filling a water bowl.
She perches on the lip, leans down,
follows the waves I make when I
settle in, trills at them to slow.

Watching her, eyes green as a sliced
avocado, I consider
pushing her off for hygiene's sake.
If our roles were switched, I would not
drink from a tub of bathing cats.

But I like her there, her white neck
stretched over my knee, disturbing
the still water with her quick tongue.

Picasso's *Woman with Yellow Hair*

Over coffee her lover sketches her.
Sloth fingers tucked in the curve of her arms,
cradled in her own mass, asleep:

She perches with a child in a paper boat,
both of them peeking over the thin rail,
watching Picasso's head on the pillow.
Then they are in Paris, at the beginning,
in front of the Louvre. She's linked arms
with Van Gough's postman, who is tall and blue,
bearded and gentle until she lets go.

The click of his cup recradled in the saucer.
She opens her eyes, peers past her arms.
His face still bows over hers. She's caught,
immense and moony, in the frame of his journal,
his name a brand on the tablecloth.

SEAN ENNIS

I'll Tell You What I Do Know, Ricky

No luck taking her shirt off
while she's smoking a cigarette.

I tried it once, Ricky,
and you just have to wait it out.

If you do get it off, don't get sad
when she calls you Scott

because she still has feelings for him
and it probably just slipped out.

A good way to ruin dinner
is to ask who the fuck Scott is

because honestly, Ricky, you don't
want to know and she will tell you.

If her friends throw beer caps
at you, just get out of their way,

even though it hurts when they say
they thought you'd be cooler. They're just drunk.

If her old goateed boyfriend threatens you
be as flattered as you can

without getting punched. Don't grow a goatee
and don't ask if that goon was Scott.

If her firefighter dad is drunk
and wants to slow dance with you

at her cousin's wedding, do it
because after that, you're in.

If her Lutheran pastor dad suggests you sleep
on the couch, and kisses her

more than you do, don't sneak up to her room
even if she calls to you down the steps,

sexy in her childhood pajamas,
because if he found you, it would kill him.

If her dad is dead
be good to her and good luck.

And no matter what, Ricky,
know—and I'm telling you this

because you're my best friend,
and heard these stories before

and we laughed but it's not funny—
no matter what, you and her

are this close.

Endoscopy

They dropped a camera
through your guts, and I,
of course,
am jealous.

You wore a bad sort of lingerie—a tissue
with a hole for your head—
gave a wave,
and then they closed the door.

There would be nurses,
but male nurses were a possibility,
watching you with your mouth open,
full of their tubes, your insides on TV.

I paced the waiting room like a city.
What would it be?
An old man with cancer
offered me a cigar, but I refused.

Finally, the doctors came
out, snapping their gloves, jerking them off
with teeth. "Congratulations!" they said,
"It's nothing."

Just stress, our old familiar. Simple
stress. Everyone in the waiting room
gripped their stomach aches
tighter, and then we left.

Back on the street, you were stoned
and lost, suddenly in love
with your outpatient date,
a drug whose company you liked better.

I guided you back to bed,
a dud missile in a peace-time parade,
heavy and kind, where you dreamt
of the hard kiss he gave you

on the arm—bruised already—
turning muddy as a high school hickey,
and the furniture watching you
as you sleep.

Bad Rep in a Small Town

Ever walk into the GAP,
look down, and get embarrassed to realize
that, somehow you're wearing khakis
from the GAP even though you thought
you never shopped there?

So you understand the situation:
an entire town as inadvertent,
public confessional. Four bars
that make a box, hidden cameras
and mics, laugh-tracks.

Even worse are those editors/
priests. Reality TV was invented here
200 years ago on porches, in taverns,
churches, between rows of cotton
where now there's a GAP.

But people are just reruns we watch
over and over again with that 20/
20, though we're myopic as hell,
and focusing our cameras
in strange, unflattering angles.

But isn't there comfort too
when the salesgirl at the GAP
already knows your size and suggests
your next purchase, like the bartender
who thinks he remembers you,
but pours the wrong drink?

BETH ANN FENNELLY

When Did You Know You Wanted to Be a Writer?

Mal baby-sat just the one time for my older sister and me,
but I've thought of it often, strangely often, and each time I do

I'm lifted onto the warm motorcycle for the ride that's lasted now
for thirty years. My mother, home early, found Mal straddling

her boyfriend, him thumbing her nipples the way a safecracker
works the tumblers, such pant-pant-panting they didn't hear

the door, my mother's gasp. Mallory, who went by Mal—
which even then I knew meant *bad*. But fun; *the funnest sitter ever*

I'd whispered as she kissed me night-night . . . *Never again*, my mother
vowed over morning cornflakes. *Inviting her boyfriend over—*

imagine! Never again. Is that why we ratted, why we told Mom
about the motorcycle—because there we had nothing to lose? My
          sister,

forever in trouble, was glad to see someone else deep in it. And I?
I was the good child and wary of secrets, but that's not it either,

even as I began unfurling my verbal tapestry, I knew I should stop,
and could not. I told of how, our bedtime nearing, *Love Boat* ending,

Brendan pulled up before our picture window, swung his leg
off his motorcycle, and how Mal ran to where he was tilting it

on its kickstand, and how Julie and I barefoot in white nighties
followed into the June heat where the engine ticked percussion

to the cicada's mating song. Did we ask, or did he offer?
I remember being lifted up, set down, clutching Brendan's shirt,

my left cheek pressed against his back which smelled like a man,
like cut grass and sweat, the motorcycle coltishly leaping forward

and kicking up gravel as we pulled onto the road, the mailboxes
falling behind us fast, then faster, my hair blown back as if yanked

by an angry brush, and the asphalt rising as we dipped, too fast,
into a turn, and how we righted and kept on, above us strange

black scissors swooped, these were not birds I knew, not crows,
not sparrows—*Bats*, yelled Brendan over his shoulder, *Bats diving*

for mosquitoes, all my known neighborhood alien to me then,
sucked back into the gray and shuddering wind. *Bats*, my poor mother

repeated the next morning at the table where we'd eaten potato salad
hours after Mal took it from the fridge, where Brendan winked, slid

his hand in her jean pocket, where Mal urged before putting us down
way past bedtime, *Don't tell your mother*—too late, too late, pretty

Mallory, first casualty of my crafty pleasure; already I was gathering
scraps of phrases, weaving my story of someone gone bad.

Cow Tipping

I think I did it three, four times, at least—sneak out, ride
with some boys in a truck to a farm, hop the fence with our flashlights
and Coors while the small frogs fled the machetes of our feet,
crash through grass to where the Holsteins clustered, slumbered,
grass-breathed, milk-eyed, high as my shoulder, weighing a ton
and worth a grand: they'd topple with a single, bracing shove.

The yoke of their shoulders thundered the ground
and we'd feel it through our feet as we ran, whooping,
me nearly wetting my pants with adrenaline and fear—
those cows could toss me like a sack of trash, snap my bones
like balsa, though mostly what they did was roll to their stomachs,
shake their stupid heads, unfold their forelegs, heave-ho to their feet.

By then we'd be racing home, taking curves so fast
we'd slam against the doorframe, turn up the Springsteen,
me on some guy's knees, dew-slick, grass-etched—
another pair of white Keds ruined—check me out, puffing Kurt's
menthol Marlboro although I didn't smoke. Cough cough.
I could end this by saying how I ran with the boys and the bulls

and no one ever harmed me. I was a virgin then, stayed that way
for years, though I wore Victoria's Secret beneath my uniform skirt.
And no one ever harmed me. But I'm lifting off in a half-empty plane
which clears a field of cows, the meek, long-suffering cows,
and from this heightened window I can't understand
why I can't understand why whole countries hate our country.

Because of our bemused affection for our youthful cruelties.
Because the smug post-prandial of nostalgia coats the tongue.
Because despite the planes clearing fields of cows and flying into buildings
full of red-blooded Americans, it's still so hard to accept
that people who've never seen me would like to see me
dead, and you as well. Our fat babies. Our spoiled dogs.

And I, a girl at thirty-two, who likes to think she was a rebel, who lifts
like a crystal this tender recollection every few years to the bright window
of her consciousness, or lobs it into a party for a laugh—*Cow tipping?*
I've done that—who brags (isn't it a brag?) that no harm
ever came to her—what would they make of me, the terrorists
and terrified? Wouldn't they agree I've got it coming?

I Need to Be More French. Or Japanese.

Then I wouldn't prefer the California wine,
its big sugar, big fruit rolling down my tongue,
a cornucopia spilled across a tacky tablecloth.
I'd prefer the French, its smoke and rot.
Said Cézanne: *Le monde—c'est terrible!*
Which means, *The world—it bites the big weenie.*
People sound smarter in French.
The Japanese prefer the crescent moon to the full,
prefer the rose before it blooms.
Oh I have been to the temples of Kyoto,
I have stood on the Pont Neuf, and my eyes,
they drank it in, but my taste buds
shuffled along in the beer line at Wrigley Field.
It was the day they gave out foam fingers.
I hereby pledge to wear more gray, less yellow
of the beaks of baby mockingbirds,
that huge yellow yawping on wobbly necks,
trusting something yummy will be dropped inside,
soon. I hereby pledge to be reserved.
When the French designer learned
I didn't like her mock-ups for my book cover,
she sniffed, *They're not for everyone. They're*
subtle. What area code is 662 anyway? I said,
Mississippi, sweetheart. Bet you couldn't find it
with a map. OK: I didn't really. But so what
if I'm subtle as May in Mississippi, my nose
in the wine-bowl of this magnolia bloom, so what
if I'm mellow as the punch-drunk bee.
If I were Japanese I'd write about magnolias
in March, how tonal, each bud long as a pencil,
sheathed in celadon suede, jutting from a cluster
of glossy leaves. I'd end the poem before anything
bloomed, end with rain swelling the buds
and the sheaths bursting, then falling to the grass
like a fairy's cast-off slippers, like candy wrappers,
like spent firecrackers. Yes, my poem
would end there, spent firecrackers.
If I were French, I'd capture post-peak, in July,
the petals floppy, creased brown with age,
the stamens naked, stripped of yellow filaments.
The bees lazy now, bungling the ballet, thinking
for the first time about October. If I were French,

I'd prefer this, end with the red-tipped filaments
scattered on the scorched brown grass,
and my poem would incite the sophisticated,
the French and the Japanese readers—
because the filaments look like matchsticks,

and it's matchsticks, we all know, that start the fire.

Not Knowing What He's Missing

The old poet writes importantly about the hungers.
About Brahms, being greedy for intensity, hot
sunlight on small weeds, fierce honey from hives
abandoned far up the mountain. And the women,
their flavors and flaws. The places he's had them,
Paris, Japan, dire Copenhagen, stony islands in Greece.
And now he is eighty, and wishes to be in love again.
Sometimes his wishes sound like bragging.

She reads his poems gratefully in her small
Mississippi town. It's an undramatic life, yet
these past months she seems to have found the intensity
he yearns for. This also sounds like bragging,
though she doesn't mean it to. If she could, she'd let him
bear her secret. She'd let all the great men bear it,
for a few hours. Then, when she took it back,
they'd remember how it feels to be inhabited.

Last night the secret kicked her awake. She grew
hungry. She didn't want to roll-heave out of bed,
but the secret demanded. She walked to the kitchen, stood
eating handfuls of cereal from the box while the birds
sang in the dark. Remembering what a racket
birds can make. Finally, the secret was content. She tried
the bed again, facing the rising sun. The secret kicked
so hard the mattress shook, but the husband didn't wake.

The Kudzu Chronicles

—Oxford, Mississippi

1.
Kudzu sallies into the gully
like a man pulling up a chair
where a woman was happily dining alone.
Kudzu sees a field of cotton,
wants to be its better half.
Pities the red clay, leaps across
the color wheel to tourniquet.
Sees every glass half full,
pours itself in. Then over the brim.
Scribbles in every margin
with its green highlighter. Is begging
to be measured. Is pleased
to make acquaintance with
your garden, which it is pleased to name
Place Where I Am Not.
Yet. Breeds its own welcome mat.

2.
Why fret
if all it wants
is to lay one heart-
shaped palm
on your sleeping back?

Why fright
when the ice
machine dumps its
armload of diamonds?

3.
The Japanese who brought the kudzu here in 1876
didn't bring its natural enemies,
those hungry beasties sharpening their knives,
and that's why kudzu grows best
so far from the land of its birth.

As do I, belated cutting, here without my blights,
without my pests, without the houses or the histories
or the headstones of my kin, here, a blank slate
in this adopted cemetery, which feels
a bit like progress, a bit like cowardice.

Kudzu quickly aped the vernacular—most folks assume
it's native. Thus, it's my blend-in mentor, big brother
waltzing in a chlorophyll suit, amethyst cufflinks.
When I first moved down south, I spent a year
one afternoon with a sad-sack doyenne in Mobile

and her photos of Paris, interesting only because of her hats—
ostrich feathers, ermine trim, and pearl hat pins—
Oh, no, I don't wear them now, they're in the attic,
full of moths, wish I could get rid of them,
she said when I asked—and I, green enough,

Yankee enough, to believe this, said I'd like them—
and wherever I went after that, the Spanish moss
wagged its beards at me repeating her judgment—
pushy—that took a year to stop smarting—Hey lady,
where I'm from? They called me exuberant.

4.
I asked a neighbor,   early on,
    if there was a way
                              to get rid of it—
Well, he said,
                  over the kudzu fence,
    I suppose
                  if you sprayed it
        with whiskey
                              maybe
    the Baptists would eat it—
then, chuckling,
                          he turned
            and walked back inside his house.

5.
September 9 and still so ripe
bread molds overnight,
mushrooms pop up like periscopes,
trees limbs wear hair nets—
really the frothy nests of worms—
men have athlete's foot,
women yeast infections,
and even on Country Club Drive
they can't keep the mold
off their cathedral ceilings

6.

Isn't it rather a privilege to live so close to the cemetery that the dead can send us greetings, that the storm can blow bouquets from the graves to my front yard? Yes, the long spring here is beautiful, dusk brings its platter of rain to the potluck, and the centipede grass is glad and claps its thousand thousand legs, oh once last May I flung open my door to the rain-wrung, spit-shined world, and there it was on my welcome mat, red plastic carnations spelling MOM.

7.

Odor of sweat, sweet rot, and roadkill.
                         I run past this slope of kudzu
                                        all though the bitchslap of August,
run past the defrocked
            and wheelless police car
                              (kudzu driving,
                                    kudzu shotgun,
                                          kudzu cuffed in back),
run past these buzzards so often
                  they no longer look up,
                        tucking black silk napkins
                                    beneath their bald black necks.

Sweat, rot, and roadkill—and yet
                        the purple scent of kudzu blossoms.
                                    After a while, other perfumes smell too

simple, or too sweet.
            After a while, running these country roads—
                              one small woman in white,
                                          headphones trapping
the steel wail of the pedal guitar—
                  one forgets the kudzu's
                        avalanche, and that's
                              when it makes its snatch—
                                    turn your head to catch—
then it holds its hands
            behind its back, whistling.
                        Juan Carlos Garcia RIP
                              is painted on the road.
If you need to dump a body,
                  do it here.

8.
Nothing can go wrong on a day like this,
at the county fair with my friends and their kids,
and we're all kids wherever there's a 500-pound pumpkin,
a squash resembling Jay Leno,
fried Twinkies and Oreos,

kudzu tea, kudzu blossom jelly, kudzu vine wreaths,
4-H Club heifers and a newborn goat which peed like a toad when I
lifted it,
we're all kids drinking lemonade
spiked with vodka, strolling between the rackety wooden cabins
waving our fans, "Jez Burns for Coroner" stapled on a tongue
depressor,
then milling around the bandstand
where every third kid in the talent show sings "God Bless America,"
where the governor kisses babies,
where later The High School Reunion Band
makes everyone boogie from shared nostalgia and bourbon
and where
why not
I'm dancing in front of the speakers
and let the bassist pull me onstage, where
why not
I dance like I do for my bedroom mirror
Behold I Am A Rock Star
I cross my wrists over my shirt front, grab a fist of hem in each hand,
act as if I would shuck it off over my head
just to watch my fans go wild

I love Mississippi

later I tell D and A about it and they say
Neshoba County Fairgrounds
wasn't that where the bodies of the civil rights activists were dumped?

Like the kudzu I'd stroll away, whistling,
hands behind my back,
like on a day when nothing, nothing can go wrong

9.
> When I look back on Illinois,
I see our little house on the prairie, the bubble in the level. I see
> tyrannical horizon, each
solitary human pinned against the sky less like a Spanish exclamation mark
> than a lowercase i.
One had perspective enough to see the ways one's life was botched.

> When I look back, it is always
winter, forehead cold against bedroom window, below me the neighbor's
> shredding trampoline
offering its supplicant eyeful of snow month after month after month
> to the heedless white carapace of sky.

> It was either
the winter of my father's slow drowning in liquids clear like water
> but fermented
from the dumb skulls of vegetables—potatoes, hops, and corn—

> Or it was the winter
deep inside my body where my baby died by drowning
> in liquids clear like water
cut with blood—for weeks I walked, a tomb, a walking tomb.

> In the heartland I remember,
it was always winter, and if spring came at all it came like a crash of guests
> arriving so late
we'd changed into pajamas, thrown the wilted party food away.
> The western wind we'd waited for
hurled an oak limb, like a javelin, through the black eye of the trampoline.

> It's not fair, my mother claims,
to blame a state simply because each morning Sorrow patronized my kitchen
> and stood behind my barstool,
running her bone-cold fingers through my hair.

> But Mama, Sorrow
hasn't managed to track me here. Strict, honest Illinois: No more.
> Let me grow misty

> in mindless Mississippi,
where, as Barry Hannah writes, *It is difficult to achieve a vista.*
> You betcha.

10.
Is that why we fuck so much?
Because we're so hot to the touch?
It's too hot to think, too hot for the paper
your fingers sweat through, we're deep
in the dog days so why not take off
early from work, why not take off
the this and the that,

what's a little more sweat from a bottle of Bass,
what's a little more sweat from his hand on your ass,
why not stop, drop, and roll, why not climb up on top,
what a view of the moon, what a nice little pop,
arf arf—
arf arf—
arrooooooooooooooooooo

11.
Am I not a southern writer now,
Have I not walked to the giant plot the kudzu wants but is denied,
Have I not paused to read the brass historical marker,
Have I not marked the twenty paces eastward with solemn feet,
enjoying my solemnity,
Have I not trod lightly on those who lay sleeping,

Have I not climbed the three steps to the Falkner plot, raised as a
        throne is raised,
Have I not seen his stone, the "u" he added to sound British,
affecting a limp when he returned from a war where he saw no action,
"Count No Count," making his butler answer the door
to creditors he couldn't pay, offering to send an autographed book
to pay his bill at Neilson's department store
because *it will be worth a damn sight more than my autograph on a check,*
Have I not also been ridiculous, have I not also played at riches,
Have I not assumed the earth owed me more than it gave,
especially now that he lies beneath it, under this sod blanket, this
        comforter,
in *the cedar-bemused cemetery* of his own describing,
Have I not stooped beside his gravestone and sunk my best pen into
        the red dirt,
leaving it there to bloom with the others
beside the pennies, the scraps of lyrics, the corncobs and bourbon
        bottles,
because we often dress our supplications so they masquerade as gifts,
Have I not suspected Faulkner would scoff at this, at all of this,
but have I not felt encradled?

12.
Common names include
Mile-a-minute vine
foot-a-night vine
cuss-you vine
drop-it-and-run vine.

Covering seven million acres,
and counting.

Like the noble peanut,
a legume, but unlike the noble peanut,
forced into guerrilla warfare—

•1945: U.S. government stops subsidizing Kudzu Clubs
•1953: Government stops advocating the farming of kudzu

•1960: Research shifts from propagation to eradication
•1972: Congress declares a weed
•1980: Research proves certain herbicides actually cause kudzu to
grow faster
•1997: Congress declares a noxious weed

Oh you can hoe it out of your garden, of course,
but, listen, isn't that your phone?
Take heed, blithe surgeon,
resting your hoe
in the snake-headed leaves, then walking inside.
The leaves disengage their jawbones—
cough once to choke the hoe halfway down,
cough twice, and it was never there.

13.
When I die here,
for I sense this, I'll die in Mississippi,

state with the singsongiest name

I remember, at five, learning to spell—
when I die here,
my singular stone will stand alone

among the Falkners and the Faulkners,
the Isoms and the Neilsons, these headstones
which fin down hills like schools of fish.
I'll be a letter of a foreign font,
what the typesetter used to call *a bastard.*

And even when my husband and daughter
are dragged down beside me,
their shared name
won't seem to claim my own,
not to any horseman passing by.

Listen, kin and stranger,
when I go to the field and lie down,
let my stone be a native stone.
Let the deer come at dusk
from the woods behind the church

and let them nibble acorns off my grave.
Then let the kudzu blanket me,
for I always loved the heat,
and let its hands rub out my name,
for I always loved affection.

ANN FISHER-WIRTH

A Confession

"And you too, God—you are ill with me."

That was a bad BLT day. Full summer, when the magnolia leaves hang leathery, cicadas scrape at my brain with their incessant crescendos of chanting and whirring, and sweat stinks up my underwear so bad I need to shower three times a day. And exhaustion sets in: I'm like Scobie's wife in *The Heart of the Matter*, I just want to lie beneath a mosquito net and whine.

So when I made BLT's for supper I didn't toast the bread, ciabatta, which was soggy. I overmayoed the bread, and used overripe tomatoes, and undercooked the bacon. My husband got pissed, really pissed, because he too is living in a climate where the underwear is rank and the blood sugar is zero. And he said, *I'm not going to tell you this is a good dinner, and I'm not going to eat it.*

I slammed off in the car, and drove out of Oxford toward the Waterfowl Refuge, seeking dark, seeking silence, when a deer came bounding into the front wheel of my Honda. I felt the thud, I sickened, there was the *gimp leap gimp leap* of the tormented animal as it lurched bounding away across the fields, and back across the lightless road that ran alongside kudzu and beaten-down trailers.

Now the front of my Honda is dented where the hot flank hit it. Swear to God, I couldn't do but evil in the Mississippi summer.

Army Men

1

Isaac, for whom I prayed, is back from Iraq.

My poetry student three years ago, before he left
he said, *I joined ROTC for the scholarship,*
why else? The Marines made him a pacifist.

He's different now. One eyelid twitches,
small as waterbugs' ripples on still waters.
They're crazy, they love to kill each other...
He picks up his spoon, lifts soup

but doesn't eat. *We slept on the ground,*
didn't wash...we drove around, filled in
wherever they needed us. He's jumpy,
starts to eat but lets the spoon drop.

When Katrina hit I got my 100-gallon
water jug and drove on down to Biloxi.
We lost it all but I was home
in the wreckage and death and nothing.

Just like Iraq, it was great... The muscles of his face
tighten, the way roadkill bare their teeth
as the flesh dries. *I'm not a pacifist anymore.*
I've done things that I'm ashamed of.

2

I'd like to say I don't understand him, but I do.
You do what you gotta do, he says.
When I was small, my Army father showed me
how to kill a man:

surprise him from behind,
wrap your arm around his neck,
and then *Crack!* he'd pretend to do it to me,
push up on the jaw, and *There goes the neck bone.*

For years, I dreamed my father
lurking through darkness with his billyclub,

sneaking up behind, then *crack!*-ing bad Koreans.
Or hacking at jungles, guarding prisoners.

Or locked up in a Quonset hut, chained
and tortured for secrets, with only a bowl
and a concrete floor. I was sure
they would find a twin for my father

and send him to Japan to join us.
My mother would be fooled, accept his gifts
of garnets and pearls, never know
he was locked up somewhere.

3

One photograph, and others: My father
in Korea, hair slicked back,
skinny and kind, the science geek
in his khaki winter uniform and glasses.

And on the internet today: faces of little girls
eaten with white phosphorus.

4

My father never talked about his wars.
I never saw on his face that tight
jumpy snarl with which Isaac seems to glance
into brutal efficiency, into someone screaming.

But my mother said, when she picked him up
at the Omaha train station, Christmas '45,
she found him alone on a bench
at the far end of the room, huddled over,

head in his hands. She said they just looked
at each other for a while, not speaking,
silence gathered around them there in the train station.
I asked her what was wrong.

If you don't know, she said, *I can't tell you.*
And she told me it took months
for the telegram to reach her,
the telegram he sent to let her know he was returning,

because he addressed it, simply: *Home Street.*

5

What do I know? Not much.

As a child, I leapt to my feet
whenever I heard "The Star-Spangled Banner,"
climbed from the car to stand at attention
at Taps while they folded the flag.

In the basement in the '50's, Pennsylvania,
my father kept his billyclub. Somewhere,
his rifles and pistols. In his bureau,
the dogtags, the medals for marksmanship.

He wrote us stories about a dog named Pinkelfritz
and a dog named Fritzpinkel
and a cat named Kitty BlueRibbon, from Seoul.
He shined his shoes every Sunday morning.

At the end of World War II
he screamed, once, in his honeymoon sleep.
But my mother told me that. She also said,

on the road to Manila
he could smell the bodies burning.

Three for Mr. Keys

1.   1970. Emmett Till
In suits and two-tone heels, the mothers
lined up at the back of the room
to supervise. Outside the international
school, barges heaped with coal
labored up and down the Meuse
past slag heaps, past pollard sycamores,
slick wet roads, clod-gummed fields,
and towns built of slate. And the students

who had never heard "a Negro"
listened to Mr. Keys
as he told them the history of civil rights.
An hour a day for a week they bent
their shining heads over pencils
as the guest speaker from back home
talked to them in his voice that rolled
like a river. And the mothers hovered nervously

lest he tell what they called a biased story—
Mr. Keys, principal of a one-room school
in south Louisiana, who couldn't keep his job
if he didn't get a Master's, and couldn't
get a Master's in south Louisiana,
so the man whose life he'd saved
at the Battle of the Bulge
helped him get a Master's in Liège—

Tonight I entered the library in Oxford,
Mississippi. A boy in a special exhibit,
big as life, shot in black and white,
strode grinning toward me.
No one had hurt him yet, this boy
Mr. Keys told us about in the final hour:
Emmett Till. His flesh as warm, as radiant,
as the flesh of those long-ago seventh graders.

2.   Mr. Keys
The night of my party to celebrate
the triumph of our school's experimental
Civil Rights Week (because even the mothers
agreed that Mr. Keys "had handled himself
with dignity"), when I cooked tacos
for thirty-five students and turned the volume

floor-shaking loud on "She Loves You"
so the kids could jump around in our
seventh-floor apartment that looked down
on the star-shaped flowerbed
surrounding the statue of Charlemagne—

When I went up to Mr. Keys silent on the couch
and tried to coax him to his feet,
what I learned was that he didn't
want to dance with me. But I was his hostess,
in my flowing hippie dress slit to the thigh,
and I begged him "Please, Mr. Keys,
don't be shy," so he steered me
till the end of the song
like a chunk of wood through a tiny box-step.
Now I consider his home, where to put
his hands on *the white girl* could mean death.

3.   Then, April
In his brown cardigan and father shoes
he sat in the parlor of his friend's house,
looking out over fields spiked with green
beneath a Flemish sky. His friend,
a quiet Belgian, gave us coffee.
The light grew pale and a chill came
to the early evening. Mr. Keys had got his Master's.

Mr. Keys would go back to the peeling
beadboard building where the water faucets
leaked rust and half the books
bore some other school's DISCARD stamps.
I have seen them, since, these schools
with their shot steps rising from red dirt,
not much better than burned-out buildings.

But back when I was young, I thought
he would be happy. Wanted him
to be sad at saying good-bye to me.
But he just said: *I'm tired.*

When You Come to Love

When you come to love,
bring all you have.

Bring the milk in the jug,
the checked cloth on the table—
the conch that sang the sea
when you were small,
and your moonstone rings,
your dream of wolves,
your woven bracelets.

For the key to love is in the fire's nest,
and the riddle of love
is the hawk's dropped feather.

Bring every bowl and ewer,
every cup and chalice, jar,
for love will fill them all—

And, dazzled with the day,
fold the sunlight in your sheets,
fold the smell of salt and leaves,
of summer, sweat, and roses,
to shake them out when you need them most,

For love is strong as death.

JOHN FREEMAN

Loose Ends

—He knew the image of the flow was not the flow…
Jack Butler, "The Lost Poet"

Along the outer bend, the current slows
    to a lull, except where swirls gather
        around a jutting stump.
    Here is a good place to stop
and contemplate the river. Who really *knows*

what he knows, beyond some facts, when perceptions change
    each other, when conviction and doubt
        argue, when one boat's
    backwash struggles with another's?
What I search for is the faculty to arrange

this body of water slipping past, to solve
    the loose ends of the field equation
        for All. I toss a stone.
    Like echoes, a few creases return
intact; the ones going out dissolve

in greater waves. I can't recall the name
    of the man who created Chaos Theory,
        but I see each separate wing
    of a billion butterflies fanning
shock waves. Perhaps it is the same

law when a red giant's core explodes:
    through a lens what looks like smoke rings
        erases its planets, but scatters
    a field of new stars and spins
into the void its jumble of roiling codes

our radios intercept. I launch my share
    of turbulence into whatever
        holds it all together:
    one step, another, I walk away
through ripple upon mangled ripple of air.

Age

Driving home from work by the shortest route
I slump at the wheel, laboring like a clunker
with carbon-fouled plugs. Roads are longer
than they used to be; the minutes, by far, shorter.

In my living room windows the silhouettes
of trees vanish into a darkening sky.
I lie back on the sofa, bend my knees,
lumbar muscles relaxing their mortal grip,
and focus on the ceiling's blank screen.

    I used to leave the roads with names
  and turn onto dirt paths. I bumped in ruts
     of abandoned logging trails
    till grass brushed the oil pan.
On foot I'd enter woods shadowy with omens:
    bubbles breaking the still surface of creeks,
   paw prints in mud, snap
 of leaf or twig on the ground,
     shivering bush.

    And I would cross to the far sides
    of hills, probing deer trails beneath the dark
weave of branches, twisting through brush and vines,
  till I encountered
     clearings where winds chanted
   in strange tongues, the solemn robes
    of willows rippling, and light burst into auras
that hallowed the crowns of oaks and spilled through fiery grass.

    But this was never enough –
  I came to slopes where naked roots
of scrub pines clutched the soil, and a longing
     clawed the red clay at my core.
  I plunged into the next thicket to search
the hidden place where light would never stop rising
    to fill my dry gullies like flood water.

Now, stretched on cushions that sink beneath my weight,
I am pulled under by the gravity
of sleep. In the shallow light of dreams, I turn
onto dirt roads, the hymns of the wind rising,
on every leaf and blade a strange burning.

Cleaning the Garage

My wife finally demands it—too much clutter.
So this is how my life accumulates—
residue in dark nooks:
tattered mop and broom
with the straw bent almost sideways,
a tray of unused Christmas ornaments.

    Beyond the open garage door
brown oak leaves begin dropping
       as death in the wind rises among them,
   pulls this one, that one, making more room.

Not everything is junk—motor oil, cans
of touch-up paint, my toolbox,
a/c filters, potting soil and trowels—
but the rest? Neatly stacked
posterboards for the shelves I haven't built,
a warped checkerboard with maybe a dozen pieces,
a broken-handled wicker basket.

And then *this* box: some mimeographed sheets,
old texts and roll books
from classes I don't remember,
my silkie's (dead six years) rhinestone collar
and "I Love Daddy" sweater,
my City League softball glove. How can she
expect me to break their grip?

    Out there a leaf writhes
as the wind reaches to tear it loose.

The Chosen

Out for a walk along the back roads
under the cloudless blue eye of autumn,
something turned me aside—I hadn't noticed
before this oval slackness in barbed wire
from countless incursions into this neighbor's woods.

Beyond his fence I found a path where sudden
rustling of disturbed wings and branches
alerted me that the portal was watched by vultures.
I entered a green realm murky as twilight,
the way strewn with blossoming snakeberries,
amanitas, coils of poison ivy,
harried by mosquitos and yellowjackets,
haunt of the rattler and black bear. The path
played out, but I worked my way through undergrowth
that snagged at my legs, grasping vines, and webs
strung from leaf to leaf

   and eased into a clearing—
     among scattered saplings
and broomstraw tawny with fall
      a lone massive oak.

   Late afternoon sun streamed
      through the woods' edge, elongated shafts
from stain-glassed windows, patches of straw
       lit like clusters of altar candles, the golden
    hush solemn as an empty cathedral.
Out of the still grass a dove rose, its white
  underside aglow in the sun's rays.

Then came the voices, or was it one voice
      formed of a hundred voices
    ululating in a single rapture?
An explosion of crows released by trembling branches, each
     the shape of an utterance,
      the sound of the heartbeat's speech,
  the dark of the earth reaching up to the light.

It was over. Whatever Presence
had waited here for me was gone. I was left standing
in an open field of strawgrass and saplings,
before a tree, nothing more.

I retraced my steps through forest gloom
darker than before, and wedged through gnarled
grapevines, around fallen trunks
shrouded with saprophytes, the path humid
with decomposing leaves, aware of the crunch
of broken twigs, nightmarish screeches.

A brightness glimmered beyond an archway
of trees, expanded as I neared it, until I emerged
on the road home in the sun's last radiance
burning along the crests of distant hills.

DAVID GALEF

Lusus Naturae

"Stay out of that patch! That's fireweed—
It'll burn your hand," my father said,
Pointing at a thicket by my shoe,
The green stalks tipped with glowing red.

Another time we came upon a ledge,
Seamed like an old woman's face.
A spry brown root filled the cracks.
"Take five years, might take ten,"
My father tapped the face with his stick,
"But granite-buster did all that."

We walked along the meadow's edge,
Viewing someone else's lambs.
They all stayed away from a tipsy flower,
Low to the ground and butter-yellow.
"That's sheepsick, that's why," said you-know-who.

My father taught me all he knew
Of blossoms and stray blind growths:
Creepy crawler that clogged dirt roads,
Jimjam berries that tasted of punch,
Queen bee with its purple-black plush
Against a field of gold.

I retrace the paths, aiming to recall
All that he taught me on random walks,
From green and white crocodilly teeth
("Good for digestion") to a growth
On a log: a brown, yellow, and orange
Mixture that he carefully labeled "stew."

I loved the names from out of his mouth:
Raven's down, bearded lily, spider's teacup—
But did I love my father, too,
When I found out he'd made them up?

It's all right, I guess.
I've been lied to before.

And now I'll tell a truth of sorts.
I grew up in the city,
Where the only thing that grew
Was the brittle brown grass
Fringing the sidewalk cracks.

My father?—an office accountant
Without any knowledge of botany,
So I had to invent him, too.
The strong brown father who
Took me for walks has mostly gone.
But I still love the names.

Town in Pontotoc County, 1935

J. B.'s Café sits crooked to the church,
The Pentacostal with its whitewashed spire.
Hardy's Hardware has a new screen door
With a hand-lettered sign, "MULE FOR HIRE."
Coldsoil Real Estate shares its office
With a painless dentist named McGhee.
Sykes once practiced law in that boarded-up house
Next to the lightning-split cedar tree.
Dan's Feed 'n' Seed has burlap sacks
That haven't moved in over a year.
The Planters' All-State Union Bank
Is built of granite and rests on fear.
Jim's General Store is plagued by flies
That buzz the most when business is slow.
The county jail hosts one old drunk.
It's dusk. The buildings' shadows grow.

M.L. HENDRICKS

NewsStarWorldPostDispatch

The Hyperboreans live
on the other side
of the North Wind, where
it's always warm and sunny
and feathers fall
instead of snow. But

Calumet Farms sold
at auction. Afterward,
for dessert,
floating island.

In gray Baltimore,
an eleven year old girl
finds her mother and little
sister murdered in their apartment.

Chunks
of cliff stranded
by erosion.
Matador Beach, Malibu.

"These eyes are the eyes
of a woman in love,"
inside the television
Marlon Brando sings.

When the Trinity and the Brazos
flood the cemeteries,
caskets pop up and
float like boats. Away.

On the Christmas card you
sent, the three of them—
the lion and the lamb together
of course
but an angel walks
between, her hand
on the head of the lion.

Daddy O

I turned out good looking
Like you.

I've stepped stones
in a mossy creek,
slid screaming
into cold water.

Danced in heels, turned
in tempo like a fine
rhyme, my skirt
sailing high.

Smoked cigarettes,
drunk wine in dark bars
and wondered,

twisting
cars fast
round curves
and smooth,
about you.

Turned out good looking, but
my eyes
aren't yours.

The photographs,
O Daddy O,
Have your never old eyes gray,
hair curly,
and square-jawed face.

I look not
knowing
what to look for.

Sister

-I-

You
frowning into the sunlight,
face a study in concentration,
three years old.

We stand close
beside the tree with
the swing,
posing sternly for the camera
Daddy holds
waist high
a few feet away.

You: brown corduroy trousers
white tassels on the front.
Me: a checkered shirtwaist dress,
saddle oxfords.

Frowning, more serious then as now,
you saw
how silly we were.

Another photograph:
in ice blue satin
perched on a folding table,
you're Tiny Tot Queen,
drinking Orange Crush,
fussing women pinning your tiara,
smoothing your skirt.
Your mouth a smear of orange,
your eyes on something far away.

At two, impatient,
you marched on the
tops of your curled-under
toes and yelled "Stupid!"
as you followed me through the house.
Precocious.

-II-

It has been a summer like
that summer when
we reached full height.

Air-conditioned apartment
and hot parking lot,
endless back and forths
just to feel the change
on our forearms,
a prickling.

Sitting hunkered on the stairs,
halfway up in the dark
we said, "You're getting on my nerves," still
awkward then, with nerves. We imagined them
firecrackers. "Pop" say the ganglia.

Long restless days of
magazines, TV, Pop Tarts,
and trying on each other's clothes.
Once, I chased you up the stairs with a kitchen knife,
intent on murder.

We looked in the mirror
for signs of something good,
and out through
the dusty upstairs window to
spray-painted names and words
on the overpass,
past the carports and the
flat pane of the swimming pool
to the place where the sun fell
out of sight
behind a dirty cottonwood tree.
Always looking.

Watching in the almost dark
the nurses and the Corvette boys
straggling toward their pastel doors
all boomboxes and towels
and suntan lotion—
Trying to imagine it.

-III-

January
and we are stumbling down
the stony creek bed behind
your hill house.

Grabbing at grasses and scrub trees
along the banks
to keep from falling,
hair white-spotted with snow,
we leave chill fingerprints
on lost drainpipes and
spills of concrete. You show me
the rock balanced mid-stream,
the tiny winter flowers
horizontal in cracks where
their earth has tilted.
Then
red berries iridescent against bare branches,
the stillness of an open field,
the wide-cheeked cliff face reflected
in a shallow pool.
You show me birdlike
raccoon tracks and the prints of deer
you have seen
not a quarter mile from your house.
There is more, but the snow falls again, harder,
until a white opaque depth
is all there is,
and we go back.

Climbing wet and cold to your house
where the men are waiting.

JOHN OLIVER HODGES

Great Legs

　　　　She loves my legs, always complains
about how great my legs are—so long, so shapely, so
　　　　strong, so great. "Not a ounce of
cellulite," says she, and we walk, because
　　　　legs need walking.

　　　　This evening, we don't walk through the
skate-park's lot to the waist-high rail
　　　　that separates it from the sidewalk.
For she'll never let me trick her that way
　　　　again; women in skirts ought
not be seen straddling splintery wood rails.
　　　　"I'll teach you to hop over it," says
I, but she blames her legs.

　　　　Now here comes a barefooter with blond
hair and a stubby boy; they traverse the grass, arriving
　　　　at the waist-high rail. The barefooter looks
for places to cut through, and my companion feels
　　　　vindicated, says, "See, I'm not the only
one," but the girl—her legs are long and thin and bare
　　　　all the way up to her tiny little puny little
shorts—grabs the rail with both hands, straddles
　　　　it modestly, brings her other leg over and
basically makes short work of the waist-high rail.

　　　　T'was very elegant the way she did that, but
the two of them now are in front of us, the girl's
　　　　legs on fine display, both muscular
and dainty, a white girl's taperings the color of light
　　　　honey, and shaved, no cellulite. I look away,
but where else to put the eyes? Of her legs she is
　　　　proud, unlike me of mine. Each leg beckons,
though not through lust. She can squat without
　　　　tipping, spread without ripping, do back flips,
I'm sure. So limber and lithe, so solid; but the
　　　　unmussed bottoms of her feet look tender,
those arches that speak, with each step,
　　　　white girl, *white* girl.

Now, when I wonder why I saw them,
those feet bottoms, so very well, I discover this: she
        had a special way of walking, each foot
peeling longly from the walk. Whoever would've
        thought she was showing them off? See me
with great legs in my house, imitating her special
        way of walking, finding her out.

        When she and Stubby ran out of sidewalk,
onto the blacktop they did go, her legs in relief; they
        crossed that black sea to a Jeep Grand
Cherokee; and we, my wife and I, walked on, and
        were at the corner when the light went
green. That's when they passed us by, and the
        barefooter's dainty hand raised just for me,
a kind look on her face, a gentle wave
        to a man more than twice her age, a salute
from one pair of great legs to another.

On Telephoning Barry Hannah from Alaska

To pick up the phone and press the buttons, what
magic, those numbers, a combination of what
the cat brought in, in a good way, but what
a mess I am, terrified, a fraidy cat, what
the rat brought in after being chased. The what
the man makes is why, the brilliant answer to why
make the effort. Will I try to go where
there is only room for one? A Mississippi crossroads
to shake a deal with Absalom's ghost? With my
finger poised above the phone I tremble, but bravery
descends and I string together those numbers and call
him, from Alaska to Mississippi, hear the jingle once
and again, the sound interrupted mid-ring by softness,
the voice of the wife of the genius, who speaks as
if she knows me, but the flu is in the house,
she says, and Barry is unavailable, but she'll have
him call me. Do I hear children in the background?
A turned-on TV? Is the genius in bed sick with
a fever? I'm thinking he should not call me, piddley
person that I am, so I say this weird thing: "Maybe
when the flu has flown I should try again," and
she, the ex-model I've read about, she who works
at the museum, forecasts Friday, and I thank her and
think of myself as the cat who chased the bird away.

MELISSA HOLM

Miss

You could sail the Mississippi to get to me,
slide down the country on your back,

your palms a cradle for your neck
and your ankles taking turns

as you cross and uncross your legs.
And you could think of me,

the honey I keep on my tongue
for you, the nickname you gave me

(so original, I've let the next one call me the same.)
Mel—honey in Latin, sweet and syrupy,

I will never go bad, I will last you a lifetime
and then some. But Wisconsin has changed you,

isolated and acrid.(The name is a mistake.
The English mispronunciation of a French

adaptation of an Indian word. *Ouisconsin.*)
It is an appropriate place for a relationship

graveyard, like you, a mistake. So tell me,
did you misspeak? Did you mean to lure

me to that place with false promises
and make all your words a prefix meaning

badly, wrongly, failure? Instead, I moved
to Mississippi (father of waters, great river,

gathering of waters) to regain the parts
of me you eliminated only to be called "Miss"

(named for lack of a man) on a daily basis
and finally on the phone you say you miss me,

casually, like you missed the 12:05 train.
You've already caught the next one, the next girl,

made her your new mistress. I call you back
to say I am sorry I missed you

that time I threw the glass tea jar, that time
I tried to catch you in the icy driveway.

When you sail on your back down that river
with the name that makes you think of me,

tell me your story when you get here
and leave nothing and no one out.

Letter to a Dead Husband

I am learning what life is like without you. Independence Day was last
week, and I watched gold and white litter the night. The wind carried
the remains, raining dust, showering the crowd with an ashen sky. I
was grateful. It has not rained for sixty-three days, not since before
the morning I found you on the kitchen floor; the refrigerator door
yawning open. . . Life is stifled. The grass and those garden tomatoes
we planted are burned. The neighbor's noisy children stay cocooned in
air-conditioned rooms. The weatherman predicts an Indian summer. I
now understand the paralysis of that woman from your work (Shelia?)
who lost her three-year-old in the backyard pool. Do you remember?
The next morning, she said, she just stood there and stared at the
track marks of his fingers in the butter.

JAMES CLINTON HOWELL

Field Rations

My sister Cristy and I rummaged Dad's rucksack
whenever he came home from Ranger School
or missions to Finland teaching farmers to make
cannons out of plastic pipes, aerosol, potatoes.

From the clink of backup bolt assemblies
and copper bullets shinning in his broken field kettle
we wrestled loose his leftover rations: superdry fruit
sealed in olive-drab foil, food in uniform.

Cristy slumped out of that canvas pantry and
sneered a package open with her baby teeth.
I unfolded the vacuum-packed wrapping
at the corners first, like turning down a perfect bed.

Mummy peaches and bananas sponged fast
from dust around our tongues. In a bright room
across the house, mother-father stuff crackled free—
baby brother an apple secretly plumped.

Gunkanjima Pen Factory, May 1952

A conveyor belt stitched from kimonos
of those who died in the war clatters
ballpoints down the line.

He draws one from the flow
to snap on a cap then put it back
but stops, stunned by the pen's
black vein.

> Between the wars his mother's father shows him how
> to dive for quartz clumped under reefs atop hot currents.
> His first time down he gropes three glints within a coral rift
> and holds a wolf eel's teeth—
> > slamstrokes to the flat blur sky
> and passes through a cloud of shrimp. Rostra stab his chest
> to welts. Air bloats from his lungs.

> His old man rises from the waves, quartz and eel in hand.
> The boy blinks vomit and salt.
> > By firelight he wrings heads
> from shrimp, flicks limp sandveins into embers.

Pen husks, clear as silicate,
clog the assembly line.
He snaps down black plastic
light as discharged rifle cartridges.

T.R. HUMMER

Mechanics

Now I begin again to refuse to say the things
I have refused to say all along:
How trucks on the turnpike raise a seizure
Of passage, a spasm in the plywood walls
Of this room where we lie in refugee heaps,
Too many for the pair of ruptured beds;
How venetian blinds slant radiance down on us
Like sea-illumination falling on certain fish
That mate only in this precise incidence of light.
One of us is a father: a crowbar
Of neon touches his sleeping face;
His peace is the stillness
Of the crushed after the bonemill lifts
Its powdery wheel. One of us is a mother:
She lies on her side between him and the wall,
Awake, expecting the shift
Of the sprocket. Many of us are scattered
Bodies of children, some ratcheted
On the second bed, some on the floor:
Dreamers less made of flesh
Than of one anothers' names, driven to this
Bedroom stained with the rainbow
Of factory oil and the darkness that beats
At the world from inside the lower
Chambers of the heart of Christ. Hours
From check-out time, the sleeping man
Makes an anonymous sound, a perfect glottal
Echo of 1957, martinis, Edsels on the freeway,
Eisenhower's golf swing, yellow Formica, the residue
Of Korean mortars showering down in the cheap-
Motelroom-cover of night. One child on the floor
Wakes up. His mother took him sleeping
From the back seat of the whipped-out Chevy,
Undressed him, laid him down. Now
He finds himself wearing only his faded
Underwear, and he shivers and whines
For the first time with his own peculiar shame
At the thought of his naked skin. The mother
Stares at the window as if she could see

A world beyond the chemical light that leaks
Through the blind-slats. She slips out of bed
And covers her crying son with a sweater.
Something moves in the mirror's half-darkness.
The shape she sees there could be anyone's,
Living or dead. She thinks she does not care
What the dead are doing. She knows the dead
Do nothing, exactly like the rest of us.
They are all on their way somewhere else.
None of them have jobs. This is the only transfiguration
Any of us here can understand: Three days and nights
And the money will be gone. By morning already
Light will come down harder, scarring us
With unconscious brilliance, burning. But now
The woman feels a tingling in her hands
Where she touched the shrapnel-
Gashed flesh of his belly years ago in the silence
Of a bedroom like this one, and started turning out
Poverty after poverty, each granting itself
The luxury of an *I*: Every stroke of the piston bearing
Body after laboring body in
To the emptiness we call a living.

Scrutiny

After the D&C, she stood waiting for a taxi
In the clinic awning's shade. It was afternoon in her
Comfortable little city, early rush hour. She could hear
Traffic beginning to swarm under a bloodless bisected moon.
She was watching everything with singular attention,
Men in their wrinkled suits and skin eclipsed by sweat,
The iridescent black of grackles in the gutter, the bright
Chrome and yellow of a 50s Lincoln at the stoplight,
The ambiguous look on the face of God, the shape of her own hands.
And people looked back at her, she thought, with more
Than casual regard, neither sentimental or curious,
But as if they had something disembodied
In common with her. Suddenly she understood how acts
Of attention corrode the world so the flesh feels scraped away,
Worn thin by the action of light, by the eye.
Suddenly she desired another life, a parallel dimension,
Translucent like our own, but in which the dial of consciousness
Is rotated one counterclockwise click, so every mind possesses
The body immediately to the left. At the corner of Second Avenue
And Royal Street, she paid the driver. He watched her as she vanished
Up the steps of the brownstone, a dominion he will never enter,
An allegory whose other side is blankness.

First Assembly of God

What was it, crosstown, where the bluesman blew riff after riff
And rattled his cup on the curbing, moaning, that made you
Snatch off your cap and look up there, mouth open, breath in the steel
Air of Chicago childhood rising like a Sunday School image of prayer?
You were the one I loved then, the way I wanted to love

Girls on the tenement steps, bums on the corners:
With a godlike purity I no longer understand, an oceanic feeling,
Everything taken literally. It was you who saw it first. How can I tell you
I have long forgotten your name when your image is with me always, uplift
Of chin, pulse in the neck, strong line of nose in profile, cap crushed

In one hand against your heart, looking up and pointing?
Three storeys over the street where gangster cars and sepia horses merged,
It glared its bitterness, red paint strafed against brownstone,
first assembly of god. You see how it all comes back, like music: 1934.
We walked those freezing Saturdays needing the bodies of men,

Wanting heat, wanting work. That year there was sweat in the factories,
Sweat in the dark of the slaughterhouse and the groins of the fathers.
And there we were, whatever our names, useless and broke on the street.
What were we, ten? In some other life, I tell you how much I want you
To lower your hand and turn to me. But you pointed up,

You stared, you said *So that's what Protestants do,*
And told me the vision it gave you, an angelic assembly line
Where hieratic ranks of the proletariat hoisted their shining tools
As enormous organs and limbs made their way down the belt, God's body still
In its elemental forms: primitive elbow joints, ur-vertebrae, eternities

Of nerves and pipelike capillaries wound on miraculous spools, the greasy
Rush of furnaces in the tunnels of the small intestine,
The lobes of the liver and the mirror-image lobes of the brain
And the circuitry that connects them, the host of crated hands
With their isinglass nails, the nipples in Cosmoline, bolts, the oily nuts,

The inevitable genitalia broken down and packed in excelsior and silk,
All bearing for the first assembly. *My god, there's work for a man,*
You said, your face with its wind-chapped skin alight with the living blood,
And I thought of the only Jesus I loved, the icon on my Russian uncle's wall,
How the holes in his hands wanted grommeting and the port in his
side wanted seals:

I looked down the street where the first of the marchers lifted
Under the hammer and sickle their *Workers of the World, Unite.*
I wanted to kneel in front of you, I reached for your arm, but you were gone
Into the crowd on the sidewalk where the bluesman's "Love in Vain" was lost
In the noise of boots on concrete, sirens, horses and drums, O brother,

Son of dust, cog in the wheel, archetype lover, man.

Friendly Fire

*Land war will require the most complex
combat flying ever flown, with more
tragedies of friendly fire inevitable.*
—CNN newscast, 2/4/91

Heraclitean, for instance: the world as a gaseous
Shimmer, like afterburner fumes in the oily night sky
Outside Carbondale, where lovers pass through the flux
Of the heart's napalm—or alchemical: the transformative image
Of the sun over Dallas, antiseptic if you could touch it,
Tritely ætherial, the volatile gold of gas-well burn-off
On the freeway's horizon, cauterizing, uncorrupting bone—
We could imagine anything. Suppose we pulled a lever
And every carburetor in Charlottesville
Detonated in a transcendental rush of mustard gas
And oxyacetylene? What would we think we were seeing?
What residue would remain?
                                    I think it would be elemental.
I think it would be pure. I think it would give off the smell
Of brass, chrysanthemum, caustic old velour—
Or that strange metallic odor that drags my grandmother's face
Up from the flare of my neurons, where the innocent dead all go:
A bombed-out country no body belongs to, untouchable, chemical, clean.

The Heavenly Doctor

Against phthisis. Against hysteria, scoliosis, quinsy.
Acute to the rhythm of the womb's trepidations, morphology of rupture,
Circumcision, leeching, the inhaling of chloroform during labor.
Indentured to disease and infirmity. Dedicated to radical cure.

Against chronic bronchitis and laryngitis: opium smoke.
Against neuralgic affections and rheumatism: the same and again the same.
About death, nobody knows anything, no matter what they tell you.
In Milan, they say a corpse can be consumed in twenty minutes

By a stream of hot air at white heat, for about $3 cost – nothing left
But a little heap of snow-white ashes: As when the meteor passed
In the early morning, and, fading, threw
A sudden glaring into my room like a flash from a hunter's firepan.

Against delirium, the mirrors and smoke of the will.
Case of parturition, ordinary, $50 or more.
Administering an enema, $5. Bleeding, $1. Cupping, $2 or more.
Administration of chloroform during surgical operations, $5 or more.

In this world, saws and the fever—in the next, gauze and morphine.
Against gangrene: amputation. As on the day
The Wadesborough Bridge was cut down and the Spencer Tucker Bridge
Was burnt by order of Colonel Miller, the military commandant,

Whom may the Devil confound for the act.
There on the embankment we found a dozen or more
With inconceivable wounds. I sawed off five arms and six legs
While dragonflies phosphoresced in the breeze on the river

And twelve white herons made the astrologer's wheel in the air overhead.
Against beauty. Against all that beauty portends.
Against any fool who believes in free will or an afterlife.
Against Mysticism, hedonism, Stoicism, Episcopalianism.

Against heaps of undifferentiated flesh rotting in the sunlight.
In *The London Scalpel*, the world's highest medical authority,
I have read the following, given as an infallible cure
For smallpox and scarlet fever: sulfate zinc, one grain;

Foxglove digitalis, one grain; half a teaspoonful of sugar; mix
With two teaspoonsful of water; take a teaspoonful every hour.
It states that either disease will disappear in half a day.
It states that if countries compelled their doctors to do this,

There would be no need for pesthouses.
Against all such desperate lies, however well-intentioned.
Against nature, corruption of the flesh, the body's subversion.
Against philosophy, which is nothing but the history of our fragmentation.

Against fatherhood, patriots, pride of war, saber and Minié ball.
Against the human race, which could have ended millennia ago,
Or in any age, by radical celibacy, if everyone on the planet
Would but accede to it. Against knowledge, physical or metaphysical,

Which leads to nothing but this: The soul is flesh. Do as little as you can.
Vis cogitativa, the power of sense: Watch cloud formations change.
Vis rememoritiva, the power of memory: Don't turn your back on your brother.
Brimstone fumes kill every species of fungus in plant, beast, and man.

Case of abortion, actual or threatened only, $25 or more.
Case of syphilis or gonorrhea, $20 dollars or more *in advance.*
For the blind poor, Rx: bleed. For yourself, Rx: love nothing.
Sow rows of onions only. Plant turnips in the dark of the moon.

JULIA JOHNSON

The Woman in the City

She waited, driftwood body stung by wasp,
her folded hand like a knife. She was irritable, too
lifeless to wait any longer. The radio rattled and she
remembered her stroke in the stream. She turned like a top,
in, and then once out, she was bright as golden hair. The
trees bristled in the open air. She looked back, the orange
of her dress like an unpredictable peach. Her thumbs held to
her shoulders; it was twelve o'clock. She worried about
something other than her hands. They had helped her,
she knew, in the brassiest and smallest way. The breeze died
down around her smooth head.

Motet: Five Voices

It's not for you
to recognize as you wander up
the path, a fury of bees
making its way into your shirt collar.

If what you already know
is remembered, in an instant,
is fixed on the brain, then you will
take instructions: Play now the violin, wand on string.

Note how the counting of time
and the door of the hand give you reason
to keep going. How in the birth of these
voices the slow breath keeps breathing.

The fire around the bend holds its heat.

When, over the hill, a tree trunk takes
a dog-head shape visible, your legs stop
before you do. You think you have folded up
on your bed, but you have gone out, into the shadows.

The Band of Spring

We cannot investigate the shadow's makeshift silhouette, a tipped
hat, a hand on the hip, a bag as large as a globe, moving across,
just beyond the yellow ridge.
We cannot, old now, breathe shallow into the heated tribute:
We call out loud.

A long course to the bright sky, hemmed in awe.
In separate rounds, beneath tents of skin, we shake pictures
from our eyes, see things, even and clear, and hear
because of the sounds they make.

These are the findings of the band of spring.
These are fat, whirly bulbs we hold tight
in our fists, holed up in the crisp cabin now.

The Rabbits

I have a habit of losing rabbits in my sleep.
They hop out, leave their baskets behind,
following me in the distance with their thick, ragged fur.
They are leading each other in a row
like a string of pearls lining the hill.
But I will lose them. The night will grow gray
in their eyes, like heavy sheep in heavy dirt.
I hug my last rabbit.

O from the road's rocky curb,
I am the marrow of a rabbit.
I will wait for them, turn over, count.
These rabbits will soon beg for me back, backing up the hill,
white blur across a tilted screen.

The Kitchen of the Sleepless

No one left in this spacious room.
This is the best place to sit.
A kettle's whistle drawn to a close,
soup finished shaking in the bowl of a spoon.
The light has nothing,
except a chair to rest on.
Spare the gestures. Nothing to show.

The birds outside on the sill
call their faintest call.
I am still here, my hands empty on the table.
And I lose track of what sleeps,
the stove cracking, breath against the glass,
this room stirring in its own space.

LARRY JOHNSON

The Capture of Weldon Kees

And so, Juan Robiños, after thirty years
The hand fell on your shoulder and you whirled,
Gazed into sungreen eyes, gold hair, and thought
My drowned daughter would have looked like this—
And there they were: tequila in one hand,
Books in the other, and lower, at khakied hips,
The nine-millimeter automatics. *The jazz!*
The jazz, you thought. It was all a trap.

Indeed it was—Coalcomán was not
A town for jazz, or anything but rum
And scrubby palm trees, cactus juice, and salt
Crusting over the sand like a glass's rim.
How many days had they played before you heard,
Before you came down this one street and found
The lime-painted cafe, and felt the chords
And entered—and why didn't you flee
At once, seeing the tall, tanless blonde
(Her virid oceans of eyes)—too haughty-clean
To be a tourist—and the little band
Too kempt, well-fed, their faces turned away
As they skreeled jazz outpristining your conceit.
Behaving like someone in your own poems
You ordered a drink and listened to the sax
Call you to ascend a desert of light
Toward dry, clear eternities . . . but then
You turned your back—and the hand clamped and held.
Magenta blood that Rimbaud strangled up
Before his death had crept for thirty years
Closer, each sand grain closer, and spread mind-wide
Until, transforming to a delicate hand,
It seeped into your shoulder. When it joined
Your veins it shrilled with a martyr's bliss.

The music ended while your terror grew
Into bewilderment—the band became
Six sinewed soldiers and the willowy girl . . .
They grinned for a second, then frowned. She raised her glass
(Seagreen fingernails sliding slick around it),

~120~

Childlike, and spoke softly through Dovering teeth:
"Hello, Mr. Kees. Would you like one last sip?
The autographs can wait—we have to go."
"What . . ." you blurted. "I can't go anywhere."
(Were you speaking Spanish or English?) "Who are you?"
They smiled again—saw something in your eyes:
"Alcatraz is closed, Mr. Kees," she said.
I saw it sparkle as I cleared the rail . . .
"I am Juan Robiños," you rasped. "Cobalt blue,
My last sight was realms of cobalt blue."
She purred, "Yes, Mr. Robinson died, Mr. Kees.
He drowned in San Francisco Bay at last.
Maxfield Parrish outlived him: had you remained
In our world he might have outlived *you*.
We're here to take you home for trial now."
You thought—what kind of weird guerrilla band
With 1984 behind them now
(What *had* occurred in America these last years?)
Was this? Were those handcuffs at her belt?
Wide kohl-lined eyes stained that creamy face
With glaucous fanatic light—what was the charge
Her pouting lips seemed about to read?
Desertion? Slipping by your death? The man
Who died in your place being your poetic soul?
(You remembered the fright when you let Robinson fall.)
Would you be punished for that murder soon,
A coward expatriate in a living shell?
What judgment was due since you had cheated death?
You pondered the worst of pain, and then because
You had heard just enough of what the world
Was like above the Rio Grande, you knew
Your fate, updated from horrors that lurked before,
Seeking to dry your life out to a page:
Critics, poets, students and lecture halls,
Interviews, readings, traveling, expectant faces,
Faces of disappointment, shreds of sleep.
No doubt their stereos and air conditioning,
Televisions, politics and smog,
Jap automobiles, tenure, credit cards
Would keep you distracted while you endured it.
Until the roof falls in, they seemed to smile.

You thought of thirty years and what you did
Without thinking of what you did, just felt.
Was this *The porchlight coming on again*?

The world and not the page? What meant it all:
Some gun running for freedom-fighting clowns,
Getting shot at once while fleeing blind
For life under a palm-serrated moon,
A little marijuana smuggled north,
Aztec relics, blue snakes from Belize,
Even a parrot business—all for free,
Each for the cells' needles of self-content
Or what the turbid body thought was such?
What had you been in this kapok of your life—
Observant, compassionate, or a sponge of sense?
Why parchment-thin children, their noses oozing flies,
Dying old men lifting some rusty cross,
One raked drop of cocksblood on your cheek,
Mudfleas and swimming pools near vague saloons?
Were jaguars real or just on muralled walls?
Was the dysentery leeched out of your ass
By pity for the cracked fingernails
That picked the leached-out corn, for the strataed rot
Of blood-encurdled, lost Tenochtítlan
Whose influence, seeping up through modern life,
Was metaphor for all you thought we were?
Midnighted under San Francisco Bay,
Its waves above flat as Nebraska's heave,
What of the paintings, bebop, photography,
Movies, green wormwood of all pianos lost?
Poetry's ganglions still entwine their grip
On bridges and water, jungles, every mask.
Had you lived with them or become a character?
Her lush green eyes seemed linked by a chain:
They both descended, flowing about your wrists.

Gold crusted sun tarnishing the street,
The Mexicans stared, even the dull police,
At your thin shape among the gringo youth—
Your hands clasped before you—shuffling north
Toward all the steel, glass, plastic. Mouldering books
Will preserve you for us, won't they? *"Wondrous life!"*

The girl's slim legs rippled in the glare. . . .
You felt no irony. You desired none.

Red Skeletons of Herculaneum

Yes, lady scientist who glues my shards
together with such ease, I was a slave:
those lesions in the bones of my upper arms
told you that, made when muscles shredded
(how I shrieked) that day I had to carry,
ten years old, my infirm father's load
of dead gray firewood, brittle as my red limbs
pitted from lack of calcium, as you see:
at twelve my skeleton shuddered as I was pressed
into soft ground by the humid, enshrouding skin
of older, sunfish-odored male slaves
using me thoughtlessly as my owners did—
but still engraving in me the pang of life—
till very soon the mistress took me in
to care for her daughter, that child you found in my arms:
downy yet shrill and never caring for me
she spit in my face once, but as we ran
from the waxy chalkflocked cloud I carried her,
panting hopeless cheer through her gritty hair,
to the beachfront chambers that became our tomb:
packed in choking dark with the mouldy brass   .
stench and taste of terror I covered her,
strained to soak that aura from her pores,
tried to shield her with my scrawny flesh
as the gases seethed our lungs to crackling husks
and the boiling sludge enveloped us with the sound
of vast black mothwings beating on the sun.

Sentry

I'm the one who always dies at night for you
In all the movies, novels—even life:
Somehow the night knows but it never tells—
Knows I'm going to die yet doesn't smirk
Or shudder in a warning jest before
The cord seethes around my throat, before
The hand crimps my scream and blackened steel
Sleeks between ribs, before the rifle butt
Stamps a spiderweb throughout my brain.
I'm legion, and each time you see me die
Failing in my duty, though I kept
A decent watch, usually, but then
Always, I nod or droop to sleep at last,
Or jerk toward that skittering in the brush
Where the hero's thrown a rock—and then it comes.
Did you ever think what my nights are like—
Knowing they're out there and no matter what
I do they'll still skulk up behind my back,
Strangling, stabbing, bashing. Hero-fodder,
That's what I am, and also don't forget
It's no fair fight—your brave warrior's only
A sneaking coward—though his mission's just.
How boring to be a necessary death!
I pray for a quick and painless bludgeoning
But anybody can swing a club; therefore,
The blade's keen scorching or the hissing cord—
Both showing off the hero's strength and skill—
Are used most often in my sacrifice
To the gods of convenience and cliché.
Perhaps I love this earth. . . I could whine
That I adore my mother and girlfriend too,
But that's no help—you won't ever stop
Heart-racing toward my death. Is it because
You almost never have to see my face?
No. I'm here because like all of us
No matter where I turn I turn my back.

For Jessica

They say your mother danced for Hitler once,
then caught the last Dutch steamer out:
I see her running now (small, lean but hard
dancer's muscles runneling skin
which the murderer doubtless admired—*so*—as she leapt),
achieving the gangplank dexterously as it rose
to liberty and her fate of meeting and loving
in bombless countryside the war-
and booze-maddened Mississippi boy
who courted poetry in vengeful Paris, destined
to combine uniquely our Southern tongue
with British imagery and speech . . .
to fail at last at living,
but not before her, who alone leavened his sad
fear, then took her bow, gauntly mapped
with those dark veins Dylan Thomas praised.
Thus he (who had met the glorious, sotty bard)
wrote three good books, lectured, and unwittingly
scarred you with too much loving while often thralled
to bourbon, Salems, or handrolled weeds and old
Baptist hangovers climbing high on fire
spewn from your grandparents, one of whom had known
General William Booth, awaiting you all in heaven.
You, bewildered in English reconstruction
and stateside versions of slick prosperity,
heard a father's bent rage strumming your guts
to beats of a harrowing drum which combined
Beatles' racket and Dad's smoky breath
into richer throbs—and so took the sticks
to flee his talent, and your own.
You finally escaped him by becoming yourself
in a penisless pounding of *this is what I am*,
a poem-flinging drummer—affirming beats
lounging above sleek, pedal-rhythming legs
between which lies that channel out of your heart.
I, a poet your father taught without
crushing my balls with affection or snuffling guilt,
say this: he knew (erasing Hitler's leers
at your mother's grace) the ultimate crush was love.

SWEP LOVITT

We Are Here at the Pleasure of Society

He walked around saying things
Like, "Bark like a frog."
No one questioned him, in fact
Co-workers and friends quoted him
To their amused families.
He didn't back off, "Frog that dog,"
It intrigued him to watch
The machinations of faces trying
To find meaning where there
Was none. It was particularly
Diverting when women blushed.
He told only his little sister, who
Remembered his writing
"Swepis Khan" on the cover
Of a notebook in the 7th grade,
That there will come a time
When these spontaneous sayings
Of mine will be used
As proof to try to put me away.

Self-Portrait

Jan. 2, of this year of hope,
2005. Sixty degrees in Memphis,
On the retreat that is my upstairs
Porch, me, and Lola barking
At first one runner, then another.
I'm drinking bourbon, 9:30
In the morning, I've recorded
That fact before, listening
To the CD Jeremy burned for me,
*Big John, The Devil Went Down
To Georgia,* stirring songs.
Though what I am doesn't work
For all, the odd one,
The searcher, will occasionally
Meet my eyes and become
Mine for the rest of her life.
Inside, a telephone jangles.
Looking out over woods soaked
By a night of rain, and it
Still drizzling, I give a long wolf
Howl—now, turn to answer.

ANN SHIVERS McNAIR

Epithalamion for Helen

A girl must remember she's only leaves
and blades, but never as blink and gone.

She knows it means nothing at all, and waits,
but, there: inexorably clings a *nouveau nom*.

More, a girl should know that febrile
is her only hope for sinking.

She always thought she'd sing, mouthing
froth, froth, froth.

I Rest

You and I are gentle.
We know that delicate is numinous
when nothing corresponds
to primrose pallor.

All I need is a *raison de cesser*,
to know, you and I,
with life-flush starving.

Incantation

I do not imagine gulls talk of sea breeze *blancheur*,
of imprecision and ease.

They are the false beauty of days. I am falling,
and the gulls have not sung. Falling, I tell you.

L'au-delà is merely an utterance, I am told,
old like the world is translated, in song.

The gulls pause, marmoreal, or they fly,
but here I must divert myself.

The sound, the song only they know.

MIRANDA MERKLEIN

Perennial Weed

Melon of the beginning
song. Your rind is too pale;

there is no thump
when I knock
your pot, your leaves. Grow,

stop, grow, freeze;
how do I know when to give
up? You stand

still for months,
the same withered
tips like tinsel

left blowing on a wreath,
off-season.

Desolate heath, then a lime
green fan
splits the shoot

in two. And when you do
not bloom, I harvest
you, the worm.

Demonian

The hostess opens the door,
passes a glass and plastic
plate for the goat
cheese and wafers, a toast

to the mangrove killifish!
Gorging on cud and brine.

A flitting shade, the red word
breaks through the world,
will not spin fast enough—

Flickers under the skin,
behind the lids: a slight shake
in the gait that stalks me,

flash wick of tail, whipping
from the corner of my smile.

Embodied

Construction on Main
Street again. As I veer to the shoulder
to avoid a collision, my right
tire snags a pothole
and I bounce into the middle
of the blocked-off intersection.
An orange-vested man
snaps his arm, No! Back!
before the city pesticide
truck breaks my concentration...

and I'm buzzing
through the muggy air
behind fireflies and night
bugs, whipping my gauze
wings in a blur of minimal
intention: to find a red-eyed
beauty to lie with on the rotting
surface. But some small fry's
trying to divebomb us from above
so I threaten him with my
feather bristle.

Larvae on a trash can lid, hatching
nymphs, constantly being pressured
to rake more eggs—It's too much for me.
There's something burning
in my stomach and I have to go
where the air is stronger. . .
On the porch, a small hole
in the screen, where a woman sits
on a peeling wicker chair,
with a glass of stale
zinfandel, I plunge into.

DAN MORRIS

Golden Gardens, Ballard

Low clouds mean no stars tonight
and dim back light from Seattle. This beach
is as black as the lake-calm water
of this sound resting before it re-floods
the tide pools and damp rocks, the small crabs
underneath waiting for something new
to float by when all is restored. The leftovers
of a pier are silhouettes above sand in the black air.
And what we thought was a stump of a piling
is actually moving and a couple holding close
in the dark walking back to dim fires and cars.
The only thing not calm is the air,
but it is not telling much. Everything is silent
except a freight train rolling south on its track.

Frequencies and Propagation

Inside a cabin, a silver haired man
sits next to a pine table,
shortwave radio. Voices bounce
across the ionosphere. He listens.
News of events that will not matter
to his life. In the cupboard, potatoes
form eyes and will not be eaten.
Outside, pine needles mulch
the ground soft. Wisteria drapes
like silk, rises and falls in night's
conversation. Static spills into the room
as the man tunes for a clearer song.

Mouse, Little Mouse

How it got in
I don't know. But now
it's lying next to my bed
beside my phone. I would like
to think that it's sleeping.

Through the paper towel,
I can feel it's still soft, freshly gone,
as I lay it on the counter
to get a closer look.

Thought, perhaps, it was a deer mouse
Peromyscus maniculatus. I knew them,
summers ago, as a student of Zoology.
But it's too grey and I don't think deer mice take
to the indoors. *Peterson Field Guide* says
"house mouse," *Mus musculus,*
That's Latin for mouse, little mouse.
Habitat: occasionally found in fields, but usually in buildings.
And like *maniculatus* it has a white belly.

There's no mammae so I can call it *he*
and be accurate. I wouldn't mind sharing
my space with this little guy.

Why did he choose next to my phone
to expire, out in the open? Perhaps
he just didn't want to go alone.

Mouse, Little Mouse, Eight Months Later

Eight months it has sat in my freezer
wrapped in paper towel and double
bagged. Eight months ago I
felt sorry for it, thought it deserved more
than being tossed out my window to rot
in the weeds. Eight months frozen
with no plans for defrost.

A stiff cold mouse isn't something
you show to the girl you invite over
for dinner. Unless that's the kind
of thing the girl would be into. Then,
maybe, she would want to find
other dead animals to freeze. The robin
mistaking a window for air, a squirrel
that wasn't fast enough. But I didn't
do it for the act.

He's as good as buried in my freezer.
The frost keeps building as I keep
forgetting and now it's as cold outside
as it is for him. Might as well
let him chill until April and then give
him a grave in the ground. Something
none of his family will ever have. But
they can visit him, leave flowers, remember
the good times and hope to die outside.

Love Among Ducks

—Standing on a Bridge at River Front Park, Spokane, WA

In sludge, remnants of rain two days old
and leaves that had let go four months ago,
a drake and hen slurp through. Spending
their day the way they had hoped. Slow
steady waddle, hen in front, bills dipping.
This is aged love. Quacks aren't needed.
They've done this many times before.

I would like to think this all true. This drake
and hen, together, enduring life. I would like
to think there is love among ducks
and that we, people and ducks, can be
sympathetic to the other.

And later, he stands in grass
on the edge of water, considering
distance swum, spreading feathers just right
to encourage those last two drops of water
to shed, a hope steady as breath that she
will stay happy in leafy puddles.

DARLIN' NEAL

My Arms

In a dream
I swim
with a dead woman
once friend
who taught
my baby daughter
to dance.
My arms push
The water higher
My body down.

She
somewhere above
still twenty one
appears mindless
yet conscious.

Strange
I am not afraid of her
But of how I can't understand
my arms.

In This Frame

In this frame
My fingers through my hair
A shush to myself.

In this frame
Find roses of cool metal
Curl toes around slender bars,

In this frame
Step outside into the cane, whittle for hours
Toward a whistle.

In this frame
Cut soles from cardboard for my shoes
Feel the rocks on the soles of my feet.

In this frame
Church bells in the morning
Walk a mile, ride a school bus for two hours.

In this frame
Design dresses made of air
Run tinted shimmering glass along gold lines of my jeans.

In this frame
My cheek brushes raised circles on the cover
I can close my eyes and sleep.

Blue Moon For Daisy

(1910-1999)

The night you died
Three tornadoes tore over Brookhaven
One flew over the hospice.
I stared at the blue moon
Heard you in the trees
In the grass
Still green in winter.
When they gone, they gone
And there ain't nothing you can do about it.

Wanting to be an egg lady like you
I fell backwards out of the hen house
Chickens and feathers flying
Claws tossing my hair
I held the egg up
Unbroken.

Your children had always had new shoes, for the boys, suits,
For the girl a nice dress in case of a funeral.
Did you want to lie down beside your husband again?
The plot already paid for.
You cain't know nobody, can you baby?
You might even be married to them
But you cain't know them.

The night you died I heard you from the garden,
From porch and in the magnolia
Listen! Listen to that little bird
Something's in that tree
That's bothering him.
Wonder what it is?

T.A. NOONAN

Lily in Sundress

No witch should let her death in by the door,
but she is here: a calla child in green
and white. (My daughter had a dress that worn
color; I hated it.) "She will put me in
the ground," I think, "this Lily girl." My floor
will give to her feet, fierce trees outside will lean
to shape their wood parabola; she'll core
a hole for bones and skin in planes between.

Can Lily see what I once had and gave
to age alone? My daughter's gone, and these
dames linger here like slick-tongue slugs on graves.
In mossy frills that garland Lily's knees,
I watched my daughter go, her bell-curve wave
rising, falling: the shape of arum leaves.

The Dictator of Records

If he leads a cow by stolen leash upstairs, it can't walk
down & will remain in his quarters. I've always proceeded

as if the leash has been around my throat the whole time.
He is, after all, my tea-wrangler: *Generalissimo*, husband

of this house. There was a time when he brought shells,
warm chocolate, tiny cup-shaped likes & trifles. I forgot

how his hand could slip so lightly from me to the bedside,
scraping past these strange beasts he guides through our room.

I've waited twenty-seven years for recognition of the scissors,
mismatched socks, & police states within me. Look—even now,

frogs leap from the mug's well. The cow wavers in my reflection.
Lights out; I dream of the chimera our bodies once coupled into.

Portrait of the Artist as Order *Cetacea*

I loved his hips—their bone-tangle tightness, the way they requested

charcoal. Hence my offer to draw him nude. We'd already promised

not to touch. I saved my hands for contour sketches, the softblack vine

dividing newsprint into sweeps of muscle. It's easy to forget human shape,

to remember how his voice cracked, palm imprints fresh on my thigh,

lingering. All my defenses—water retention, insulation, genetics—useless.

My body's *give*, sweet in theory. "Go home," he said. If being a whale

is just a matter of composition or the fat pulse of a four-chambered heart,

I'll rebuild myself fusiform. I can't let him see me unable to find

the necessary exit leverage. So I hold my instruments tighter.

CATHERINE PIERCE

Epithalamium

First, know the type of car the other drove
as a high school senior, late eighties. Were there
bucket seats? Red interior? You must love
that car. You must wish, at least briefly, that you
had ridden in it. Next, you must understand
the psychology of the belt buckle and the black boots.
They were chosen for a reason. Know that reason
and never speak of it. Purchase for each other
not only books and dinners, but plastic
serving trays, origami kits, a postcard from Tupelo
to be hand-delivered, unmarked. Be kind to old
photographs, but not overly kind. Know the name
of a town in Mexico where you can someday,
money willing, spend a week. Consider starting
a four-piece cover band. Consider growing
basil and/or marijuana. Know that at no point
do you have to own a) tapered jeans, b) a good blender,
c) spare light bulbs. These are your decisions to make.
Remember small parts of many days: the Amish
restaurant outside the city. The purchase of the red vase.
The bird whose cries woke you your first morning
in one bed. How you rose together then.

Domesticity

Some days I could burn
bookshelves, carve weapons
from the wreckage, drive
fearlessly past dogs and bandits.
I could rocket through towns
of dust. I could destroy
the sheriff's good name.

Then night slips around me
and the bedroom is lit
with a strand of small lights.
My body admits to calm.
I am the same size,
but still. Outside an owl
calls evenly across the quiet,
and I ride that note,
grateful, into sleep.

But this is a warning.
Someday I could drive
the car into the ocean. I could
smash the phone, tear pages
from the dictionary. I could
make threats all my life.
Don't think I won't.

Apostrophe to the First Gray Hair

O small silver rope by whose noose
I will, if lucky, hang—

You are the highway's white stripe
dividing *toward* from *away*.

The hairline fracture
on a slowly swaying bridge.

Light plummeting earthward
years after the star has turned dark.

Instinct

I woke to screaming. Outside, a raccoon
was opening a cat. The cat shrieked like a child
as red ropes spooled from its belly.
There was nothing to do; it couldn't
be saved, was already beginning
to shudder. After another minute,
it was still, its entrails steaming
in the crisp air. The raccoon
waddled away, uninterested.

This is a love poem.
It isn't about the cat or the raccoon.
It's about you, still asleep, breathing
evenly and guiltless, and me, awake
and fascinated. What do you see, sleeping?
Empty hallways, maybe, or broken
bottles, or gardens of flesh blooming
around bullets. You could pull
so many triggers behind your eyes. Or maybe
just a woman, tall, with thin wrists. How easily
I could leave you, slip on my coat and shoes
while you dream of what I can't know. So simple

to kill what we don't understand. But instead
we allow it. We sleep next to each other,
roll over at three a.m. and startle
at the weight that balances our bed. We could
spend a lifetime circling, sniffing each other out,
and then turn to meet a dark, clawed creature
we've never seen but know like we know
our bones. Nothing can alter our course. We are animals
of habit. We shut our bodies down together,
wake each morning gutted and hungry.

ALEX RICHARDSON

Casino Hospital

The nurses in labor and delivery were laying odds on gender.
They thought it "nice" that we'd waived our right to know.

Under my breath, I asked for the inside track
And they dealt me a Nursing School legend:

If the heartbeat sounds like a train, it's a boy.
A washing machine, and you have a girl.

Wanda heard, then rolled her eyes through a hard contraction,
As though I were tossing craps during her hours of reckoning.

I think it's gender confused, I said.
But the nurses had fled, Wanda grimacing as a pit boss.

Later, I found them at their station,
Studying charts like race forms.

I told them if we had a girl, she'd love trains,
If a boy, he'd do the laundry.

I told them that's what Wanda said, and I had to agree.
Still, I anted-up a dime for the underdog.

Cat Door

Belly brought a pigeon through
In the dark morning;
I could hardly scold him;
He was so proud, even righteous,
With his platter eyes, tense jaws
Snug around the limp neck,
The shut wings.
I rolled over, hoped it was a dream,
Hoped the intermittent flapping wasn't real,
Or at least that it would end.
When I got up for coffee
And returned to bed for the news
I saw it clearly:
Unpunctured and perfect,
Bloodless above my pillow,
The gift I never deserve.

Gifts

I tried joking at first,
That this one would solidify her bust
In the Mother-in-Law Hall of Fame.
Not one, or even two, but four ducks
Huddled in an Easter basket, shivering
Right under my kids' noses.
Two were mallards, nearly ready to fly,
The others yellow, but would morph
Into sitting ducks, white and fat.
It was quick, the exchange, and later,
The ducks' development. I remain
Convinced that someone fed them plutonium
While we were away.
How else to explain their mercurial growth,
Their impressive and emerging stench,
Their complete need for hours of dotage?
And still they were neglected.
My kids, who swore they would not,
Lost interest, and I with the dogs,
Embraced my neglect with bitter zeal.
I guess that is why
Lately I have noticed birds diving
At my windshield when I leave home.
And yesterday, while I folded laundry
In neat little rows, a sparrow torpedoed
Into the glass where I stood.
My wife told her mother it was beginning to cause
Marital strife, and suddenly, I started to grow as well,
Not real growth, not duck-growth,
But growth nonetheless,
In my mother-in-law's imagination:
I became the non-nurturer of my own brood.
She promised she had a better home
Lined up, and chuckled that we'd kept them
As long as we had.
I hadn't known there were options,
Just as I hadn't known last Christmas
That I would begin prematurely to lose my hearing
When Santa stuffed a drum kit down our chimney.

PAUL RUFFIN

To the Celibate

It is your choice, and no one will fault you
for choosing as you have. But recall that
beyond the magnificence of your room,
your books and paintings,
glassware and rich mahogany,
the china bath with golden handles,
the color and light and sound
that rival all nature can offer,
beyond your burning dreams of this life,
your head filled with enormous learning,
beyond the riches of this cloister,
you are bone and flesh, designed to breed
and die, no less than the purest holy man,
no more than the lowly oyster.

Frozen Over

In Mississippi I recall only once
how the cold came down like a lid of iron,
clamping the landscape, stilling the trees,
and all the ponds froze over: not
just a skim for crashing rocks through,
but thick and hard enough to walk on.
The gravel pit where we swam in summer
spanged and creaked as I edged out
toward the gray, awful middle where,
if I went through, no one could reach.

I moved like a bird coming to terms
with glass, sliding one foot, then
the other, holding back my weight
and breath until they had to come.

I could see, beyond the far shore,
cars moving on the highway, slowing,
faces in the window ringed with frost,
the little ones waving, pointing
to that child walking on water.

Burying

I found him stumbling about when the mother
died, an otherwise healthy calf, and fed him
by bottle until another cow came due, then
moved him in with her for suckling.
Third night she broke his neck.
It was a right and natural thing to do:
She reasoned her milk was for hers alone.
I found him barely breathing, head thrown
back, unable to rise for the bottle,
his eyes already hazing over. I could see
myself fading in them, backing into fog.
I brought the pipe down hard, twice, the
second time in malice: not for him or her,
but for the simple nature of things.
Blood came from his nose, his body
quivered. I dragged him from the barn.

The hole in the winter garden was easy, quick,
and the calf fit properly, but when the
first shovel of dirt struck his side,
he kicked, with vigor. I watched the flailing
foot strike against air. Nothing else moved.
There were no considerations: I did what
needed to be done. A few more scoops clamped
the leg and the earth stilled. I mounded
the grave and turned away, looking back once
to see that nothing heaved. I felt neither
fear nor sorrow, love nor hate. I felt
the slick handle of the shovel, slid
my thumb over its bright steel blade,
breathed deep the sharp and necessary air.

Sawdust Pile

A pile, they say,
will burn for twenty years,
seething with deep heat
those long years out,
cool enough on top
for weeds and barefoot boys.

Like early ice it lures
the unwary up a greening slope
firm to the foot, firm
and cool up to the very peak,
where the crust sags, gives way,
and legs, torso, and head
sink to the fierce core.

There are the tales:
Bo Simpson's horse, a pack
of pure-blood coon hounds,
Sarah Potter's little girl
all gone to a quick hell.

Out here the rattler warns, lightning
strikes from a growling sky:
each terror is given a tongue.
But the fire lies quiet in this pile,
a coiled thing, tongueless and waiting,
beneath the devil's cool shell.

Gigging Frogs

There are some things on this earth
that may be fooled by two moons,
one still as a stone in the sky,
the other dancing. Not these frogs.
A moonlit night is not a night
for going after frogs. When your light
joins the moon, their clatter stops,
the pond goes dead: they are not fooled.

It must be done on a dark and dooming night
when yours will be the only light above
the rim of the pond. You must move
with the stealth of winter with your moon,
as slow as a stone sliding across the sky.
Then, as you see the eyes take life in
a seeming joy, moon-struck, you steady
the light, aim the deadly gig, and jab
the prongs through belly or head,
swift and sure as a cottonmouth.

When you have taken all you want, you
must ice them down for the trip home,
first cutting the hind legs, still joined,
from the upper torso, skinning them
like removing too tight jeans
and laying them side by side
in the ice of your cooler,
the legs of so many lovely girls
collected by a moonstruck man
who slew them for his joy.

JORDAN SANDERSON

Homecoming

The chimneysweep's daughter feared spontaneous combustion and carried with her everywhere she went a fire extinguisher so that she might put herself out should flames pour forth from her pores.

The reserved woman's son, who made a dentist, feared paroxysms and washed his mouth out with Novocain three times a day.

The florist's father feared dead flowers and filled vases with silk
forget-me-nots.

The lawyer's well-dressed husband feared fainting and wore clothespins under his clothes so that he might always be pinched.

The exterminator's aunt feared poisoning and kept roaches in her purse, released one to test thresholds and corners, cups and quiches.

The surgeon feared loneliness and stitched her twins together at the
ear.

The seismologist's mother feared trembling and monitored her extremities with a level, its unwavering bubble the lover she could not
touch.

Blue Springs

The pools were almost too clear
To be worthy of the dares that echoed
On the banks. I stood on a ledge,
The bottom of my trunks barely damp.
She sloshed her stomach, her shoulders:

A kind of easing in.
Gasps of revelation burst
From immersed bodies.

The difference between seeing and being
Swallowed. The shiver of being washed,
Of being bathed in the washtub of the eye.

The current carried us, our bellies
numb, our faces burning.

After the late spring sun set, fireflies showed us
parts of the dark we hadn't seen before.

Oral Hygiene

To cure her toothache, we went to the fair,
rode the Tilt-a-Whirl, ate bouffants of cotton
candy. Her cheeks swelled all day
with funnel cake and gulps of root beer.
The House of Illusions swallowed us
and mirrors lined up crooked as wisdom
teeth. She was the one-eyed queen
tapped from the thick of the deck.
She counted the acrobat's toe hairs,
named each bead on his forehead. At dusk,
she said the day was giving itself to the one
million bulbs so they could light the pathways
between roller coasters and booths—each one
got a ray. We sang along to the music hidden
far behind our backs, the notes making it
seem that her tongue had never touched
the slick point of an incisor.

Elizabeth

Checking into the Moon Wink Inn after midnight
wasn't a big deal to her. Not like admitting
that she thought of the sun as a video-camera
and skyscrapers as strips of film. She never
wore panties, but every day she wore a scarf
double-knotted under her chin, a baseball cap
in summer, a black turban if she expected a crowd.

I told her once that her lipstick made a speakeasy
flicker in my mind, walls the color of sweet tea
with three drops of lemon. She said we were
getting too close and didn't call for four days.
Then, we spoke only in complete, declarative
sentences. "It is very hot outside." "Yes,
and it is hazy." I wondered what the haze
looked *like* to her, but it would have been
better to fingertip-feather her thigh than to ask.

She slept that night in a red hairnet, brown ends
protruding and I whispered into the tips as if they
were phone lines: "Peaches, Graces, Wisteria,
Ducks." The next morning I said goodbye,
and she looked at me as if I had conjured a balcony
where a woman stood with a shaved head,
lowering a single egg by pulley.

DANIELLE SELLERS

Counting Mississippi

I peeked around the doorframe. My grandma was still,
slouched in the same position for one whole day now.
Over the phone, the nurse asked me to count
the seconds between her breaths. She said
the pauses would lengthen, the measures grow faint, then stop.
At first, there were ten Mississippis between each breath,
then twelve, then nine. It was late. I wouldn't sleep.
I lay on the couch in the living room, staring
at the Memphis news, then Leno's muted chuckles,
I learned how to patch a roof, the history
of beer. Infomercials from the 80s—
I'd seen them all before.   Those Friday nights,
some fancy torte of hers would keep me up
shaking my foot and tossing my long hair,
I'd listen to her sleeping next to me.
After Dynasty, after Falcon's Crest,
Miami's news, the Johnny Carson show,
the ads began: the clapper, chia pets
and hover rounds. The late-night crowd is old,
they want to stay around.   Some twenty years
since then, in Oxford, Mississippi now,
I listened to her breath catch, thought it might be
the last a hundred times. I wanted sleep.
I thought of that weenie roast at her house
in 1987, playing hide and seek
with my Biloxi cousins—we wore masks—
Fat even then, I was Cat-girl *sans* the tights.
I hid in the foyer behind the gold lamé
mirror and no one found me. I peed myself.
She gave me clean underwear, black panty hose.
I was through with counting states, alone. At dawn
she was taking forty seconds between breaths.
Two days since her last response. I lost count,
had to wait for her to inhale again.
She wore her rattiest gown. My mother cried.
Grandma's breath became a rattled, bubbly snore.
I laid down on the bed with her. Her hand
already cold. She was technical,
administered to. The nurse slipped morphine between

her pallid gums, she was dead weight wheezing—
I counted fifty-three. She gasped three times
in short succession and no more.

Transplant Shock

After the October hurricane, after the sea
flushed the island clean of most vegetation,
I went down to see what could be re-claimed.
Not much except for what was on high shelves.

When asked what my grandmother wanted,
she said her hibiscus: five foot five
and popular with the neighbors.

Red petals, yellow pollen stamens,
its trunk forked, limbs praise the sun,
roots content in lime rock and sand.

I took Paw's rusty shovel, and dug the hibiscus up.
Now, the root ball burlaped, shrub on the bed
of my truck for three states, it's come to Mississippi
to be planted in a pot on the deck.

We learned of her cancer on Thanksgiving.
She's taken to the bed, won't acknowledge the sun
this summer. She watches *Sesame Street* reruns,
drinks orange juice from a sippy cup.

The hibiscus leaves jaundice, dry and fall off.
My landscaper says, *She might be too old
to establish herself. Don't expect 'er to flower this year, or next.*

Women in Spring

What I did not expect to, bloomed again—
those pink lantanas I planted last summer.
They did not use the same branches
but sprouted new. Today I wrenched
the tough old limbs from the bed,
with hedge trimmers that were my mother's
grandmother's, that woman I never met.
She grew up in a Mississippi orphanage,
married a man at seventeen who called her
Jenny though her name was Alice.
I wonder how many times she used this tool,
how many hot afternoons were spent
in the yard with her altheas, sweat
dripping into the secrets of her housedress.

JEAN-MARK SENS

Of the virtues of rain

take all it erases,
leaves fallen in the furrow of time

beyond printed dates on newspapers, crumpled wrappers
and the half-face silvery turn of a moon
Walking the night you are a fulcrum of your spine

balance of your shoulders, tin-thinned shadows
in and out at street light intervals
your shoes punctuate to the weight of your life
the wet pavement reflects visible stars in their attentive brightness
5 a.m. Summer pre-dawn in a fold cocoon of the rave, liquid sky light.

An old wooden table in a garden,
painted blue under a willow tree
—table to eat on an early breakfast,
sort out shells and crabs, open a newspaper,
or just lean on against the finishing slant of the day.

Dusty with pollen, dewy with night mist,
its warped top my finger coursed
tracing the shape of your name
as if letters could be the contour of your face

the rain will fill out
dimpling it to the rhythm of disappearance
giving back a glistening after-image
something of memory, filled and unfulfilled

and the rain itself
over my head to the edge of my lips,
still new in a first taste of a place.

Mississippi Owl

An owl on a shedding tree
its rimmed eyes to the moon

cold haze inside the white
its shoulderless head heaved through its tight wings

talonned to a branch it stands full face to the winds
knowing the dark counter streams where the river meanders

and field mice scurry under winter dried stalks and brambles.
A real owl all sight in the night

to the four i's of Mississippi
a Barred Owl that can see and won't tell.

JES SIMMONS

How to Survive Loss

Once the frayed tow rope snaps,
you slow to the inevitable spin
that sends you onto the shoulder,
over the embankment, tumbling
down to the hard desert floor.
Don't be too hasty to pull yourself
together, scramble for the road
and thumb a dazed ride to town.
Instead, find shade from the glare,
an outcrop of solitude and silence
to puzzle out the pieces of your life.
And though it may take years,
watch for signs of healing:
that cactus against the sun
breaking into bloom,
the mouth of that dead animal
shrinking to a toothy grin.

Witness Her Hand

The women came, drawn still
to the only man who'd respected them all
from young to infirm, adulteress to prostitute.

And with the great stone heaved aside,
they entered to find the tomb empty,
save for the grave clothes folded,

the head covering rolled, placed separately.
Surely this was a woman's touch,
straightening up before anyone arrived,

alone with the newly risen Christ
who stood joyous, stunned.
Witness her hand, so domestic and loving.

ERIN ELIZABETH SMITH

Fidelity

In the husky warmth of the Pine Belt, fidelity
is impossible. Every road leads to a home
built of sticks, of straw, and the dogs
are not wolves, per se, but carnivorous as love.
Who can hold still in this place? This bed
that opens like a curtain, the morning distant as London,

that undreamable city where you live. London,
like a memory of heat that marks the skin, the fidelity
of ghosts. Last summer, we made our bed
large with how close we slept, as if a home,
for a moment, were possible. As if hope or love
could salvage us from the dogged

winter that would follow. From the wet and bony dog
that howls on our doorsteps. From the London
fog that doesn't rise, despite how much we do not love
that shadowy unknown. It's not fidelity
that keeps a groomed herb garden, a home
as white as writer's block. It does not make the bed

so tight that one cannot slip in, the clean bed-
sheets cool as they can be lonesome. I hear dogs
wail into the crisp dark, their home
turned prison in the slumber of others. In London
you call and I'm cupped inside another man, fidelity
having run empty on the long, unlit interstate. I'm sorry, love,

but the body is a field of lilies, only lovely
when there is water and sun. Green flower beds
to root and bulb in. The strict fidelities
of a growing season. Are the flowers to blame for dogs
that bury shoes in their soil, the Londons
that are built where something might bloom? Come home.

There is still time to plant peach trees. Frame a home
that's built of brick, a chimney that draws. Learn to love
the held breath, the steady hand. What does London
have over this city? Here, we could live in one bed,
make wheat flour scones. Let in that wet, sad-eyed dog

and name her Patience. Must we always keep this fidelity
to distance, to London's ancient, chilly homes?
In paintings, fidelity is not a flower or love
or a one-manned bed, but a pale and whimpering dog.

How to Escape the South

Fill your spice rack with thyme
and brown mustard seed.

Plant tomatoes in a paste bucket,
sweeten your tea with a pale syrup.

Learn to knit—qiviut scarves
in pine green, skeins of cotton

and mohair assembled into skull caps.
Make your bed tightly. Sleep with women

you could love and don't love them. Freeze
chicken bones and celery hearts

to boil into broth. Try to forget
the cheeked key, the pick sucked

into the tongue, the turned body
sticky with salt or the girl

that looks like your disappearing city.

YVONNE TOMEK

Happiness

Consider this,
A long table with a linen
Cloth, white—
Dishes tinged with blue and
Silver spoons for the taking, and
A broth that steams with local country
Leeks, potatoes, and cream.
But add to it,
All around, on chairs or
Benches, those we love or have
Loved, or should
Love.
And on their faces, warmed
Now with, by maybe, a drop of
Wine, a drift of spring air, a shaft
Of bright light through dusty window
Panes (it is the country, after all)
And see for a moment
How they could all be living
Flowers:

> A gardenia
> A daisy
> A rose

Their skin, however swarthy,
Looking petal smooth, from the
Happiness you attribute to the
Scene. Think upon them, those

> Irises
> Snap dragons
vital
> Mums

Remember their colors,
Maybe their auras, their flower souls;
The repast is not necessarily
Long, but neither is life, as in your mind,

Perhaps, you are seeking a closing act
Before the curtain is
Drawn.

Pedagogy

Riding around looking at trees is an
alibi I give for some serious tasks—

lessons I give my child on budgeting, coping,
steering the course of daily life. But on designated
corners I slow the car and exult over that red Maple
on College Avenue and that one on Farmer or
Terrace Road, in late autumn, still so intense
of ochre, scarlet, magenta, crimson red—

my favorite time of year.

And I have been reading
Frost and Oliver and Keats,
so full they are of the revelations of autumn—
the quiet and sometimes blazing resignations—
the stillness into the dark.

And so today we are making lists and
translations, pedagogical and psychological.
Cooking tips and housekeeping hints. Fashion
statements. A little reminiscing into the archives of
family, thinking of and mentally composing
Christmas letters to write, a little gossip
thrown in. I don't understand why she
doesn't see the auras I see, though her
soul is bigger than anyone's I know,
and I tell her so.

She senses an animal, invisible to me,
in pain, for example, down the road.

"Those black branches look like the Chinese
alphabet on your red blouse," I tell her, insisting on
the beauty of some Fall configurations.

But we are so happy together.

Later, though, I overhear her telling her
father about me and our afternoon together,
as she concludes it all by saying, "We had a very
nice time together, really, but basically,
Mama just wanted to ride around all day—
looking at trees."

NATASHA TRETHEWEY

Gesture of a Woman-in-Process

—from a photograph, 1902

In the foreground, two women,
their squinting faces
creased into texture—

a deep relief—the lines
like palms of hands
I could read if I could touch.

Around them, their dailiness:
clotheslines sagged with linens,
a patch of greens and yams,

buckets of peas for shelling.
One woman pauses for the picture.
The other won't be still.

Even now, her hand circling,
the white blur of her apron
still in motion.

Hot Combs

At the junk shop, I find an old pair,
black with grease, the teeth still pungent
as burning hair. One is small,
fine toothed as if for a child. Holding it,
I think of my mother's slender wrist,
the curve of her neck as she leaned
over the stove, her eyes shut as she pulled
the wooden handle and laid flat the wisps
at her temples. The heat in our kitchen
made her glow that morning I watched her
wincing, the hot comb singeing her brow,
sweat glistening above her lips,
her face made strangely beautiful
as only suffering can do.

Secular

Workweek's end
and there's enough
block-ice in the box
to chill a washtub of colas
and one large melon,
dripping green.
After service, each house
opens heavy doors to street and woods,
one clear shot from front to back—
bullet, breeze, or holler.
A neighbor's *Yoo-hoo* reaches her
out back, lolling, pulling in wash,
pillow slips billowing
around her head like clouds.
Up the block,
a brand new graphanola,
parlor music, blues parlando—
Big Mama, Ma Rainey, Bessie—
Baby shake that thing like a saltshaker.
Lipstick, nylons
and she's out the door,
tipping past the church house,
Dixie Peach in her hair,
greased forehead shining
like gospel, like gold.

Housekeeping

We mourn the broken things, chair legs
wrenched from their seats, chipped plates,
the threadbare clothes. We work the magic
of glue, drive the nails, mend the holes.
We save what we can, melt small pieces
of soap, gather fallen pecans, keep neck bones
for soup. Beating rugs against the house,
we watch dust, lit like stars, spreading
across the yard. Late afternoon, we draw
the blinds to cool the rooms, drive the bugs
out. My mother irons, singing, lost in reverie.
I mark the pages of a mail-order catalog,
listen for passing cars. All day we watch
for the mail, some news from a distant place.

Limen

All day I've listened to the industry
of a single woodpecker, worrying about the catalpa tree
just outside my window. Hard at his task,

his body is a hinge, a door knocker
to the cluttered house of memory in which
I can almost see my mother's face.

She is there, again, beyond the tree,
its slender pods and heart-shaped leaves,
hanging wet sheets on the line—each one

a thin white screen between us. So insistent
is this woodpecker, I'm sure he must be
looking for something else—not simply

the beetles and grubs inside, but some other gift
the tree might hold. All day he's been hard at work,
tireless, making the green hearts flutter.

JOHN MICHAEL TUCKER

Shhhhh . . .

Don't tell anyone,
But Nancy's had a few too few valiums.
It doesn't show; she seems merely disinterested.
You'd never guess
That she's helping her mother suffer through the chemo,
Or that one of her professors just told her Sorry,
He wants to give his marriage another chance,
But of course he'll pay for the abortion,
Or that six days from now,
She'll suddenly start crying in the middle of
Geography class and won't be able to stop and
Someone will have to help her out of the building
And into a car that will take her to Methodist's
Behavioral Healthcare unit
Where she'll sit in a room
That's just short of a cell
And gradually get back to this business
Of seeming disinterested.
But for the next five and a half days,
She'll show up on time,
All the while fantasizing
About giving up on everything
Just to get some rest.

Counterculture Foot Soldier

Hide in front of
Every convention, pretension,
And big-budget production.

Use this glow-in-the-dark clownsuit
As camouflage.
Open your eyes, blink once or twice,
And join the cause.
Disdain your old ideals,
Conform to the standards of the Anarchists' Union,
Throw away your crown of clouds
And vanish into the crowd
Of clowns.

Unexplain with facepaint
And silver chains
The truth about you,
The person you were:
Uninspired vanilla,
Unsweetened,
Unadorned,
Certain that you were unworthy,
And now,
Underneath,
So meticulously
Unknown.

LINDSAY MARIANNA WALKER

Austerlitz and the Lost Correspondence

> *Two days after their wedding, Napoleon left to lead the French army
> in Italy, but sent her many intensely romantic love letters. Many of
> his letters are still intact today, while very few of Josephine's have
> been found; it is not known whether this is due to their having been
> lost or to their initial scarcity.*

I.
Milan, April 1796

Josephine,
There are many days when you don't write. What do you do, then? No, my darling,
I am not jealous, but sometimes worried...

I live in a mailbox.
It's a little outside the city.

There is an old man who directs
traffic at the crosswalk in front of my door

(it's a mouse hole door). He's unofficial.
Here they have stop lights already.

Someone he knows must have been run over
at the corner. I have eaten

all of the pineapple slices.
I don't want anyone to yell at me.

II.
Verona, July 1796

...one of these nights your door will open with a great noise; as a jealous person,
and you will find me on your arms.

The world has become a series of legs.
People wear nicer clothes here.

Soon I will buy boots and more cake.
That's likely to be a bit expensive.

Rêve de moi. It is difficult to be obscene
with a mailman who is not

one's own. I screwed the bookshelves
into my wall. Not much left to do.

III.
November 1796

I don't love you anymore; on the contrary, I detest you. You are a vile, mean,
beastly slut. You don't write to me at all; you don't love your husband; you know
how happy your letters make him, and you don't
write him six lines of nonsense…

You must wonder at the size of my books.
Currently they are filed between my eyelashes.

On each page a different letter.
I stole them from you, of course,

every one. There wasn't room
for us both in this can.

The Piano Keys Confess

We're in love with Ace, the janitor.
He makes our backs arch when he strokes us
with a damp cloth, solutions of warm
water, flecks of mild

scented soap. His fingers remind us
of applause. Sometimes he slips us
into his breast pocket like packs of gum.
His heart, the drum in a stand-up bass,
all the love we need. Sometimes we cry

when he forgets to put us back. Sometimes
we follow him under the stairs.

Bad Cookies

Do you have any idea what lightning would do to a cookie?

Suspected of adultery in early Mesopotamia,
you and your lover would be tied and tossed into the river.
Only the guilty sank. One more excuse for the cookie!

Red balloons on a white mailbox and mother
wagging a finger from the station wagon's window,
never more than two at a time.

There were seven different words for *cookie* in ancient Egypt—
none for *virgin.*

My cousin gives them arms
and legs. She is a doctor.

Who wouldn't want a cookie on an elevator?

Cookies in the kitchen. They fall often, roll across the yellow linoleum
          under the lip
of the dishwasher. You have to get on your knees to reach them.
          Cookies love that.

Frogs in the night-pond chirp Krishna.Oh, Krishna.
you are Cookie Monster blue.

My kindergarten teacher taught us to share ours.
She was caught sharing cookies on the roof of the high school.

The God of swing-sets
is all for cookies.

Aragoto—actor of ancient kabuki.
One tough cookie.

If you eat cookics in bed
you sleep in sand.

Cookies have extravagant attachments to old chairs and wet teeth.
A cookie sold the farm. A cookie bought the cow.

A cookie can't pray.
It waits for the refrigerator
to kick on. It chants: milk,
milk, milk, milk.

Josephine at Carnivale

Hortense and I pigeon the seaside town,
versed in trade: photos, postcards, baguettes.
The promenade gone garland with parades,
subtle mountains gray the basin, stiff as the beard
of an elder. Wasn't it February?

Hadn't the waves turned arthritic already?
We broke from the revelry to cross the level
sand, to touch that sea before we left and from the rim
we watched a bus, *Dipartimento di Scienze Psichiatriche,*

from which a group of fragile Italians in orange jumpsuits
debarked. Starched orderlies in white held hands
with the old and shy, herded each citrus slice
across the strand. *Viareggio*—Road of Kings.

One man, in a plastic helmet, face buckled snug
in the sling of a chinstrap, broke from the pack—
sprinted across the stretch. And it seemed a guilty thing
to watch—the big males chasing him into the waves.
Like the dinner party scenario where you open the wrong door

and find your host on the toilet. I have no other way to tell it.
They are not mine, the words to explain that man's face
as he pounded loose across the sand in his plastic crown, the joy
he screamed before they took him down.

Coup de Grâce

Trianon, August 1811

Josephine,
I send to know how you are, for Hortense tells me you were in bed yesterday.
I was annoyed with you about your debts. Nevertheless, never doubt
my affection for you, and don't worry any more
about the present embarrassment.

Sometimes I follow you slowly in my car
because I know you no longer love me.
You said it was for want of a window that Zhivago
deserted the campaign, Lara was all pretense.

Either way he abandons Tonya. And that's
the real problem—now I have to be a fool
for this story to work. Everything that came before
becomes a lie. Not because it wasn't true.

Isn't that what you meant? Say no,
I'll shave my head and demand more
unreasonables. I know what I look like,
though even the dogs have forgotten my scent.

My heart has two pains now: a loss and a slant.
The wolves are so thick and so
close. Mind your fingers,
you might lose one in the snap.

GORDON WEAVER

The Beekeeper's Order

Most pastimes come about by chance,
But, like a nun, I chose my veil.
So, stung, I have no cause to wail.
I've been the fool of circumstance.

And though it's existential dice,
They say, determine all men's fates,
Still, choosing what-to-do dictates
A way-to-do that's quite precise.

What's more, great nature is the source
Of keeping bees. They're born to fly,
To gather, store, to build, then die.
I, keeping, serve great nature's force.

I like my ritual—stool and smoke,
My gloves, my cotton suit, pure white,
My veil, the hour governed by the light—
The ceremony's *almost* baroque.

History adds a timeless seal
To what I do. In Europe's caves
The savages' crude painting saves
Their likeness, climbing up to steal

The honey from the gum. Wax tapers
Illuminated monkish gloom,
Preserved the flower of learning's bloom
Upon illuminated papers.

A preacher built the modern hive,
Designed the interchanging frame,
And, to his everlasting fame,
Learned how to winter bees alive.

(I find it not the least bit odd
We keepers should owe all our craft
To men who seldom laughed—
Dour Langstroth was a man of God)

This craft demands exactitude:
I cannot check just when I please
For foul waxmoth or some disease
Would decimate my wriggling brood.

My keeper's faith is in my acts:
No guesswork makes the hive increase,
Nor can regret make robbing cease.
Beekeeping's a universe of facts.

And, yet, the keeper needs some flair,
Some romance at his spirit's core,
Assistance from accrued folklore,
An unarticulated care

That renders light the keeper's hand,
That whets his ear exceeding fine
To isolate the angry whine
Of one mad bee among the band

In playing flight, that keenly hones
The focus of the keeper's eye
To trace their flight against the sky
And mark his queen among her drones.

Responsibility's the sole
Responsibility of he,
Who, alone, chose to choose, like me
To undertake, alone, the whole.

I take my honey, finite measure
Of weather, bees, and my small skill.
I love my craft, conceived in will,
That follows, orderly, toward pleasure.

My Skeletal Father

Lank leg cocked,
Rake-at-the rail, locked
In pet pose mocked
By beery belches, the shocked
Wince at whiskey straight:
A gross gutter-prate
Half-lies, half-hate.
Hitler haircut, bald pate,
Brush mustache bristles,
Tongue glints like gristle,
Coughs, curses, whistles!

Barroom smells of beer,
Smoke swirled in a smear,
A choked, sodden cheer
Of juke music jerking
Puzzle pieces lurking
In memory-mites—I, searching.

Now: no relief
From memory, mind-thief.
Fathers foster life-belief,
Mine's dying denied grief.
Broken bits strike light,
Diminish dark, dull fright,
Fill my man-long night.

Knobbed knuckleduster ring
Taps time—we sing!—
On broad bartop.
Numberless nights never stop
(in man-memory mites:
enduring endless nights!)
For chores, child, wife.

Life-night-long strife-rife,
We stumble, slide,
Saunter, stagger, collide . . .

Homeward, howling, numb.
I grasp a giant's thumb,
Guiding. Giddy, I hum
Soft songs to keep
His hells asleep.

Handiwork

for my Aunt Florence

Constructs of memory are frail, like lace
Long laid aside. Her fragile hands that made
This lace are knotted now, beyond the grace
Of craft she wrought as if she played.

Inexorable seasons quite efface
All living forms. Every bloom and boy must fade,
But her design remains as it was laid,
Quite beyond particular time and place.

It is a paradox: her hands pervade
This fragile structure, and, thus, delay the pace
At which the hand of time labors to erase
The value of this lace her fingers paid.

Auntie Flo, your handiwork spins a larger space
Than my mere words are able to embrace.

In a Dublin Catacomb, in a Retirement Condo

In a Dublin catacomb, I saw a nun's mummy,
Grinning like a girl. Her teeth were white and strong,
Her hair, they say, continues to grow.
I imagined her—or tried—a gushing lass,
Giving herself to be a bride of Christ,
Three hundred years before.

Now, I've retained much of my hair,
And most of my teeth,
But can't ignore the wrinkles' creep
And the general sag that comes of simple gravity.

I imagine—or try—the randy lad,
The cocky guy, the oh-so-sensitive fella
I liked to think I was—what is it,
Forty years ago?

I remember, or think I do, all the lovers,
And love-for-its-own sake too!
I hope I never forget
The small hell I raised!

I grin into my bathroom mirror,
I gnash my brittle teeth
And style my graying hair;
I strike such manly poses,
Snarl the latest wisecracks,
Affect a lurid wit,
And leer at all the ladies
The way a hip young guy should do.

Would that Christ
Could raise His shriveled bride
From her bed, walk her, whole and young again,
Out into that Irish light!

How I wish I'd wake from dreaming
I'm who I used to be,
On fire with lusts and love
Of living hard and fast!

The bride of Christ still sleeps
A seeming peaceful sleep,
Still smiles as if she dreams
Her lover's sure to come
And hold her in His arms.

I sneer at the old man in my mirror,
Tell myself:
Have faith, Gramps!
It is possible—I hope!—a new bride
Will come to your arms yet!
She'll love you, I say,
For your stained teeth and thinning hair,
And for every blessed wrinkle,
And raise up all your fallen flesh!

Pray for us.

Walking Through Seasons

Lady, take a thoughtful, loving walk with me.

Hand in hand, we will see
How great Nature's spring springs newly green,
How buds are swelling toward the lush scene
Of summer. Walking on, now see the bloom
Of all, Nature's bright riot that scarce leaves room
For us to pass, scarce time or need to think
This show will fade as we tread the brink
Of autumn's hand closing, slow yet sure,
Toward the clenched end of all this pure
Display that once seemed certain to persist,
Yet all the while greened to make a grist
For Nature's changes, meant for us as well.

Dearest lady beside me, can you not tell
The coming of a cold and white demise
In Nature's scheme? Do you, like me, surmise
A winter brewing in our bones, that our greening's
Long past? Walking still, can you hear a keening
That mourns our distant springs and summers, and this fall?

And yet, lady mine, if we will walk, all
May at least seem worth its loss. If we but stride
Together in a close near-dance, we can at least seem to glide
Together, toward whatever, content with foolish play and idle talk.

Lady, I ask you, what else earns its certain end so well as a too-short
loving walk?

GREG WEISS

Sentiment

Rich in fishtank and emotive jukebox,
This fetid, basement-bar terrarium
Drifts out past the blinking green and flocks
Of memories bloom. I devour them
Like the field, needlessly sequestered,
Record the dour quaver and cobalt
Whistle masochistically tethered
To the inmate. Friend only by default,
Voluntary predator of action,
He pans the solitude which I then sift
For nuggets of pyrite dilapidation.
(They flop into the water when I lift
Them for inspection.) My turns of phrase wage
Battle through the eyes of dead language.

NICK WHITE

Birthday Dinner

In Possumneck, MS, where the same old joke is told at least twice a year,
where a newly-paved highway cuts perpendicular
        across a bone-brittle railroad track,
where the library and the post office and the Presbyterian Church
        are located in the same yellow-gray building,
where after heavy rains one year,
dark brown water freed itself from the narrow boundaries
of the Big Black and the Tombigbee overlapping, swallowing, drinking-in
even more dark brown water that must have escaped from the weak earth
when we weren't looking, too busy staying alive—it
snuck up on us in the streets, vanishing the cemetery, making
little ponds out of the soybean fields in front of my house.

We lived on a hill, and the water sallied around our doublewide trailer;
we became a houseboat overnight, isolated. And looking from the right
        distance
and from the right eye, we must have been something akin to a junkyard
        yacht.

On Wednesday, the lights blinked out.
Thursday, my mother fried the last breast of chicken.
Father discovered from the old freezer that Friday aged slices of venison,
        frostbitten and grainy.
The meat hissed in the frying pan like angry cats making love and
saturated the air with a wild musk that made our eyes
        constrict and water.

The river crested on Saturday, my birthday, and mother
cooked what was left: a deer heart, plump and maroon.
She sliced it into three triangular chunks, serving me the biggest share.
And we ate the heart silently.

"We'll get by," said my father,
        touching my mother's slumped shoulder,
his red arm dripping little diamonds of sweat onto her blouse.
She forked her last bite, examined it—mushy and sponge-like impaled on
teeny
        Metal tongs—
And began to cry.
           And I was never more in love with my family.

Communion

The man in the green alb spoke of eternity in hushed whispers.
Although his words were written on the pamphlet,
His lines already plotted-out for him,
His inflection, his delivery, his tone, made them believable.
Soft light from candles outlined his thin figure as he stood
Before us; his thick eyebrows arched suddenly like wings in flight
When someone coughed, breaking the grandeur of his performance.
And I wanted to believe his little voice.
I wanted so much for the brown wine I sipped
To transform into the blood of the Lamb,
For the tortilla-thin wafers to mutate
Into the puffy flesh of Jesus.
The Baptist preacher of my childhood,
The man robed in white short-sleeved collar shirts
And obnoxious ties, would laugh at this Episcopal priest
As he quietly, in the rhythm of a lullaby,
Chanted Latin phrases that held no significance,
Except that their sounds were exotic to my inexperienced ear.
And when my turn came to receive communion,
I followed the people in the pew beside me—hypnotized by the
          romance of tradition—
And took my place at the communion bench.

"Yes, Father, I am a sinner," I echoed.

And I was five again. The Sunday school teacher drew a dot on the
          blackboard.
The chalk was the thick yellow kind that would flake off
On hands and become crust under the nails.
"This dot," she said, "represents your time on earth.
These walls that surround us only represent a teeny bit of eternity.
Things that we abstain from here, the misery that we endure,
Is just a speck of dust, a dot of chalk, when compared to God's
          timetable."

I had nodded in agreement then, as I nodded now. Head bowed,
I remembered the ravens that massed around the drawbridge
At the Tower of London. Feathered alligators hungry for
The ears of the guides, the old men who dressed like beefeaters.
I remembered how their wings were clipped because
Legend warned that if they should ever leave the Tower,
London would fall.

And I stared at these ferocious things, secretly
Longed for them to fly away from that stony prison,
To look up and find the sun blacked out by the
Hideous flapping of their wings, no longer clipped,
Outstretched in the air, feeling the whoosh of wind
Under their breasts for the first time.

Buckshot

1
Perhaps it was the acute redness
Outlining the woodpecker's crown
That first unnerved my father,
Or, maybe, it was the way it hopped
On its toothpick legs.

I remember lounging on our patio, solving
Crosswords in the newspaper, when it perched nimbly
On the plywood floor in front of me.
It must have flown down
From the oak tree to further inspect
Its reflection in the sliding glass door.
It skipped to the edge of the placemat, reading
"Welcome Home,"
And tapped lightly at the picture of its own
Knife-like beak.

Behind the bird's transparent image,
My father's hulking frame came into view,
Almost as if he were formed from the glare
In the glass, and without a sound, the woodpecker
Darted back up into the oak.
"That's trouble," said my father,
Not really speaking to me, but more to everything else.

2
My father had flashbacks of war,
Not of his actual time in combat,
But of some weird amalgamation of all wars.
Usually, it was just him and Hitler, squaring off under the
Eiffel Tower. And sometimes he wouldn't win,
Hitler would shoot him in the face, classically between
The eyes. He could see himself then blinking and exhilarated
In recognition at what had happened,
The grandeur of it all, to die in such a way.

He sometimes felt—he told me in whispers
Some evenings after we had watched the sunset—
That he could hear the ground breathing, undulating,
Puffing up with the malodorous stench of the dead.

The ant beds were always doused in gasoline;
And moles were all hunted out of hibernation.
His yard was a utopia of concrete and Astroturf.
The only things allowed to live were the trees
That were there long before he was, and they
Seemed to grow taller each year in defiance.

3
The tapping started that night. Somewhere
Up in the top branches of the oak,
We heard the woodpecker tap-tapping.
My father first thought
The sound was tiny pellets hitting
The side of the house. He tumbled
Out of bed and screamed for us to hit the floor.
Grabbing his shotgun, he went outside into
The night. And the bird hushed.

Not long after, the sound of its tapping
Became expected—a constant, especially at night.
In bed, I would listen to the combined cacophony of the bird's
Percussions, plunking in some Morse Code-like rhythm,
And the dull strikes of my father's
Steel-toed boots as he paced
Back and forth, back and forth, on the marble floor.
I began to distinguish, by rhythm
And intensity, what the woodpecker
Was doing in the elm. During the short, fast,
Angry taps, it was marking its territory.
The almost silent, timed taps were it snatching
Small insects. However, my favorite was when
It was attracting a mate: the rapping was varied and
Irregular, as if it were going insane.
It was seduction by noise, and the beating of its beak
To the crusty elm of my father quickened something
Within me that I could not quite understand.

One Sunday, after church, I was reading
On the patio when the little creature
Again alighted on the ground. And again,
It was preoccupied with its own reflection.

Maybe, I thought, it was narcissistic, seeing
In its sparse, reflected image a mate it could never have.
I reasoned that I, too, would probably fall in love

With my reflection if it were like that:
The way the smooth black and white plumage
Accentuated the breast muscles that puffed out
So proudly, the way its little figure moved in sharp angles,
The way its beak was both tender and dangerous.
The minute architecture of this thing—the vicious perfection of it!
My father had already aimed the shotgun before
I even realized he was there. The woodpecker
Was too late in takeoff. And the sound of the .12 gauge
Punching through the air pinched my eardrums.
And I fell out of the lawn chair.

4
If it were a cartoon, it would have been funny:
A bird blown to smithereens by buckshot,
The equivalent to a Mack 10 army truck
Smashing into a person, a body disintegrating
In a matter of seconds.

And my father would later laugh to friends how
Nothing was left of it but a few feathers.
How the amorphous mass of pellets hit the
Woodpecker's body in mid-flight,
Leaving little more than particles of dust,
As it fanned out into the naked sky.

BRANDON WICKS

The Failed Novelist Addresses His Fuse Box

Let's forgo the tedious puns
of blown fuses and burnouts,
of fumbling in the dark, and take aim
at the real culprit here: juice.
All the heavy, black syllables of your switches
lay unlabeled in this rusty box.
The anticipation of each utterance as they pop
makes me sweat, one by one—
nope, nope—until pausing at the last.
Not all of them can't work.
If blackouts were an everyday occurrence,
I could take solace in that. I could
pitch hard drive and monitor, floppies, zips, and thumbs,
all those metered archives of rambling ambitions,
reading kilobytes against my hours,
into a mountain of delirious spring cleaning
and be done; but it is never done.
The problem between us is this then:
an attenuated, unceasing trickle of energy
that keeps the desk lamp awake at night.
A diffuse dream in its filament
of when the house will shake with voltage,
and light bulbs would smash in their sockets.

False Imprisonment

When tuning into the courtroom drama that is my family, I like to excuse myself from the dinner table conversation, preferring instead to watch my loved ones incriminate themselves, chew their way around a history of emotional bankjobs, the tampering with anecdotal evidence, the perjurous accounts, or—as in the case of my upstanding father—the bolted door behind which the dismembered corpse of my childhood still paints the walls. It's not often we still get together, but I'd call DSS on these people, I'd throw them in the hoosegow, I'd let them hang. So then I make a show of gathering their plates, clearing their soiled napkins. It's usually here— while raking bones into the garbage disposal and seeing the wet crumbs of this last casserole we have shared disappear into the drain—that a tiny, unknown juror jumps up inside of me, moments after the final verdict has been read, and exclaims, "Wait! I've made a terrible, terrible mistake!"

GARY CHARLES WILKENS

My Easy Life as a White Man

When I arrive at a place
it's my skin that opens the door.
When I meet the people
my skin says hi.

It's my skin that pays
the tab when I run up the bill.
My skin negotiates with cops
when I speed and writes

an extra line on my vita.
My skin found this three-
bedroom house in the burbs,
it even drives me

to the ballot box. My skin
is no-nonsense, realistic
and practical. When nuts
need cracking, my skin is there.

Late in the night when
I'm alone with a flickering
candle like all men, my skin
climbs off and goes dancing.

7pm Laundry and the Loved One Far Away

Oh laundromat metaphysical,
laundromat washed in light,
laundromat place of cleanness
covered with dust.

In the laundromat of my secret
heart I cleanse you, spin you
like the cotton and tumble
you dry. You white and
fluffy again, you still warm
in my hands.

Laundromat of all races and nations,
everyone's need the same, met
the same way. Laundromat whose
only ecstasy is folding and hanging.

Laundromat windows looking
out at the rain, laundromat
like a city on a hill. Laundromat
of the sharp scent of longing.

JOE WILKINS

Letter to Paul from Sunflower

It's hot here. The air is heavy.
August has been a long scream of cicadas.
The Big Sunflower River runs swollen
and brown. In a whisper of wet fog, blackbirds
spray from my pickup, and off old Highway 49
rice and cotton give way to strangles of trees
along the bayous. They say the topsoil is hundreds
of feet thick—the rot of a continent washed over
and over again. Even the sun, just a gray ring
in grayer sky, is choked in it all. And yesterday
I saw a thousand white cranes smother
a stand of dying cypress like snow.

I stay in a small brick house on the white
side of Sunflower. My neighbors smile,
bring me big plates of okra casserole
and invitations to drink sweet tea on their porch.
I smile back, thank them for their hospitality,
and walk across the tracks, to the school
where I teach. My students are kids like any others,
but they're also poor and black and beaten
down every day by the blows of the dead,
and of the living. I like to think I'm doing
something about this, but then I cash my check
and make my way back across the tracks.

You can buy a watermelon at Lewis's Grocery
for a dollar. The big woman says, *Now, you pick*
you a sweet one. If it ain't sweet, you bring it back
and get you a sweet one, you hear? I pick
a sweet one. Children clatter across the rot-wood
porches of shotgun shacks, and the men down
King Avenue hold paper bags close to their hearts
and stare. There's a grandmother with one eye
who talks to stray dogs—this place is deep
with ghosts. Do you remember that Sunday,
driving Montana? Just the two of us, tall grass
and sky? Brother, you are far away,
and America is so suddenly old.

The Schoolteacher Blues Again

Sunflower, Mississippi, 2002

The slump-backed fish cutters sluicing their blood hand, then their
knife hand, out back of the plant in a ditch that drains to an acre
trough lip full of a day's guts; Mr. Carver, one-time freedom rider
and first black lawyer in town, shutting down his office on the second
floor of the Planter's Bank building at the corner of Lee and Evers;
the way the long fields back of Sunflower pulse like veins as the
sun goes down; my neighbor telling me she wants her kids to *be with
their own race, it's better that way*; her small daughter, all blonde hair and
smiles, peeking at me from behind the bars of her mother's legs; the
new place across town where tourists clap like idiots for mumbling,
drunk Cadillac Jackson who swallowed half his teeth one morning
when he woke to a tire iron across his face; a white rain of dogwood
blossoms on the trim lawns of the big houses by the river; the men
on buckets and cypress stumps staring through the smoke of their
cigarettes and a blood sun as Mr. Carver makes his way across the
cotton-run tracks, down Church Street, past old Freedom Hall and
Junior's Joint, dogs pissing on piles of tumbled bricks; the music
teacher down the hall whupping hell out of Orlando because too
many of the words he knows are some derivative of mother-fucker;
the private academy across town spit-shined to a gleam; the man
who owns Sunflower Food Store helping my wife to her car, telling
her *Yeah, maybe it'd be nice if they could all go to school together*, then just
stopping, grocery bags in his hands; the girl in my 4th period class
whose mother left for Memphis three weeks ago and hasn't come
back; the house fires that flap and rage like bright hearts in the night;
Mrs. Butler, who's pulled thirty-odd years of mop water across these
floors, shuffling into my room, asking *What'd you teach those children
today, Mr. Wilkins?*

Mississippi Sonnet

When you drive to Jackson in the dark,
the highway's white as old bone. Far off lights
of cropper shacks float eternally away
from you, the incredible heaviness
of rivers. You swallow the damp smoke
of burnt chaff, houses, tree stumps.
Of course someone is waiting for you,
someone with dusky hair and cypress eyes.
What songs of sadness and old rivers
does she sing? Do you see yourself in her songs?
Are you there, in a field of wind,
your back bent to the earth? You drive to her
to keep this night from shattering,
like a dry bone, in your hands.

Sunflower River Road

for Paul

This road bends around
cane swamps, raises

a thick dust to hide
the end of day. I am sorry

for my silence, ashamed
that I have words

for this road and none
for your dying. I can even

hear the green cries
of cypress trees.

CLAUDE WILKINSON

Baptism with Water Moccasin

*And the Lord said to Satan, "From where do you come?" So
Satan answered the Lord and said, "From going to and fro on
the earth, and from walking back and forth on it."*
                                                —The Book of Job

His bulk amazed us,
the way he'd maneuvered his folds
onto a switch of elm
directly above the baptizing hole.
After all, Cedar Creek offered
numerous spots for a snake
to wile away a Sunday, but only one
fit to baptize in.

Not even the brilliance
of proselytes, a rite of sheets
fluttering about them
in the early morning breeze,
had moved him. Not the most
floral, feathered, tasseled of hats,
nor the highest notes of a Doctor Watt
being held till the last thread
of their power—
nothing made him so much
as shift that bitter lozenge of head,
shovel through the chilly fork of his tongue
to even feel us out.

It was as if he already knew
what was going on, as if
he'd been returning for ages
to blaspheme the Creek.

While the deacons
crawfished into place,
one could scan the bank of faces,
almost hear people calling up Scriptures,
favorite prophets to deliver us.

The sister in the blue crepe de Chine
sees Joseph released from Potiphar's prison,
and the old man there
with Stetson still on
is remembering Daniel in the lion's den.
Over there Jonah is being spat up . . .
Shadrach, Meshach and Abednego.
Everywhere shields were rising,
going forth against the tree.

A few boys with the story
of David and Goliath
burning their hearts
gathered stones to make war,
aimed to chuck the devil down
into the cloudy waters below,
but Pastor Gamble, an old hand
at this sort of thing, cautioned,
"Leave him be, chillun.
Long as he up there,
we knows where he at."

Pastoral

Remembering the days of pear and plum
and my feeding them to our cows by hand
is heavy effort, a painful command.
After decades, I recall names of some
like Angus and Muley, the season's hum
of cicadas, songbirds, a holy strand
that wound me into the calm of the land
till dreaded mornings when rough men would come
in trucks for hauling and change everything.
Stumbling wild-eyed up ramps, cows couldn't know
their gift of paths and sweet hands was over.
Some mercy shone in those we were keeping,
but this was our way. Then times would follow
when others ambled up through the clover.

The Persistence of Memory

Decades past his power to zip
a tight spiral, yet whenever
our quarterback spots me,
after news of his latest divorce
and most recent companion,
he asks if I remember
our winning touchdown.

Nowadays, before I can smile
or nod, he's already onto
how after snagging his perfect bullet,
I was hit by the secondary,
swarmed in a moment by
their whole defense, and how
Bonehead Pye, our other receiver,
spun from his pattern, streaked
across the field and plowed underneath
an interminable tilting pile
to pull me free before
my knee touched ground.

Here is where I would have
the legend end, between
my forward progress and going down.
I'd stay there in the midst
of forearms like shivs
and them low bridging my legs,
in a more tangible misery
than the rose-colored dreams
with girls who were younger then
than our children are.

How can I tell him
I'm finding my own, different way
by the adoration of marsh flowers,
in hazy sunsets, that the best
of our best times are only
like Dali's wilting watches?

So what I do is offer
my sufficient grace of
"Hell yeah, we were smoking!"

for perhaps the last thing
on earth that he truly loves:
the part of the story where
we break loose down the sideline,
with stiff arms ready,
just Bonehead and me dashing
stride for stride into eternity.

JOHNNY WINK

The Appearance-Reality Motif

She seems a marvel from a tale by Poe
As, seated in the student union, she quaffs
The kind nepenthe of a cherry coke,
Her large eyes lost in a slender book. She coughs
In stylish fashion. I ponder consumption,
Kabbalah, decaying cities on the Rhine.
Her ebon tresses fuel my presumption:
She is a Poe girl and she's mighty fine!
Her slender volume? Alas, I am not near
Enough to get a gander at its cover,
Although I'm just as sure it's Baudelaire
As I am that she has a demon lover.
A fat guy waddles up and takes his place
By her. She belches, says, "Let's go suck face."

Generic Jam-Packed Shakespearean Sonnet: A Joint Venture

A portable pig will fit quite well, I think;
And we can certainly accommodate
A badger, villanelle, and kitchen sink,
Along with a fifth of vodka and a crate
Of plums. What's that? A homosexual?
Why not? Would you rather Baldwin or Proust?
An allusion? Why, sure! "Henpecked you all"
Will do the trick meseems, although "mot juste"
Is not chopped liver either. What? "Chopped liver?"
It's there already! Get it? Don't you see?
(I start to think that your cerebral quiver
Is sans a few of its arrows, *mon ami*.)
No, wait! I'm sorry. . . He's gone, doggone it,
And left me here to finish this blasted sonnet.

A Spelling Error

"No, dear, those sounds arrive a little later,"
The teacher thought to say—but didn't say—
In the margin of her student's final paper,
A treatise on the student's wedding day,
Which hadn't, as it happened, happened yet
But which the student dreamed—and realized—
In pints of ink, it seemed. The teacher set
Her pen down and went on: "You're well advised
To keep in mind the wedding vows come first.
Hours hence, in your Niagaran wedding cama
(Pardon my Spanish) there will be rehearsed
The change from blushing bride to redhot mama.
That setting's soundtrack will most surely feature
Those *wedding vowels* you wrote of," thought the teacher.

WILLIAM WRIGHT

Nocturne for the Second Death

At first, the wind sustains us, holds us aloft like gossamer:
the first sting of snow blown off dwarf pine
into towns that still constellate their fires,
dream and hoard the dimming myths.

To know the earth, we record expanse: meadow's longitude,
river-crux and the salt-sick coast. We search
farms of blighted corn, lean with their husks
to hear underground streams snap

and sluice dry roots into the running. To know the earth,
we record microcosm: pine needle and paramecium,
pumpkin seeds rotting in hay. Always, when moths
raid the ruined factory and chew gowns to powder,
thronging the air with larvae,

one of us will stray: Because the ice in her mouth is a lily
opening, because he leaves the purity of hunger
in a starved fox's belly, lets maggots eat the gray eyes
to a dark scald. But we are forever assimilable,
even when the lights of the earth's curve

lock all the doors: We will wait centuries for the youngest
to boast and swagger in the silence he has become,
to stitch the sky as if he could bolster the light.
He returns as the last ember's hiss,
the last frost unsheathed.

Even spring, buried in water, we keep ourselves
down with the briar and bramble. When we can't bear to be
forgotten anymore, not by sludge or sleet, we unload
the bright syllables of our hair and skin,
then move on, torches in a tomb.

Ferns

Hard to trust the way they spin and nod in the light,
always looking away.

Older than the creeks they flank, their fossil tongues
fold to the sun in green, outstretched

syllables, asking their one question. When a body passes,
they turn and glare, eyes nested deep

in their black heads. Dense and sentient with more
history than the sweet gum that seeps

and falls, or ground water that diminishes
in the fattening sun, these reversed medusas

lick through stone, outstare all the locked houses
of blood and hair, outspeak

the millennial sky-clatter of bird language, leaf-litter
and lichen, reach out, take.

Blue Pear and Sleep Paralysis

He lies reed-like in his bed as in his mind,
a lure to ghosts and master
of measuring light,

understands early how the moon finds
a raccoon's carcass under
elm leaves just beyond

the window, its mouth and intestines
ulcerated and sloughed
to runnels. A blue pear

lifted from a bowl. Minnows
prodding rain-scalloped shores, each spine
anchored for the moment's purpose.

He knows the elm is a cathedral
through which crows shake
and bend dark rafters,

leaf-light patinas on the far wall.
What is the music that falls on the grass,
retreats into the shuttered dark?

It is the man singing at the house's far end,
his mind a halved blue pear.

Fever

1.

You remember that tall Mexican
come out of the orchard
with bloody hands.
Sweat salt on his hat-brim and shirt collar.

Chewed on hard candy that looked like sapphires.
Didn't had but seven teeth.

Raked back a leaf patch: Copperhead snagged
his foot to the hard vein.

2.

All around the trees breathed on
their invisible exchanges, arborescent
heat-shimmer, light-eating leaf.

Foot swollen with venom,
he stumbled into a vision of relics
piled under his mother's bed:

(feather drum, wolf eye):

O madre,
I cup the helix in my hands
and let my faith wash through me.
I am the xylem of the Lord

3.

Engine oil guttation,
leaves greased and sagging in August heat.

Boots streaked with dust.
Head tilted back to nurse his third Sol.

4.

The truth of his delirium: her womb a cumulonimbus sac
lopsided with hemorrhage. Her brain the shell of a locust:

Hermana, I have no choice but to burn your little brown house

5.

His sister took the painting of a great storm cloud
raining from its belly a heap of red blooms.

for converting gasoline
to glossolalia, singeing the hair and the gown.

6.

Half-drunk, he ate breakfast at the PK diner
and shook his head,
claiming deafness.

Ghost Water

We enter the pond during a night of glassy corners:
Frost toughens the grass, slows red oaks
until leaves unlock. The last of minnows
like gray brushstrokes. We turn home
to see what's abandoned—

windowlight, Mason jars, blue corymbs of hydrangea,
fading like our skin that brushes past cicada husks,
snake skins, old burdens shucked. Death smells
like wood-smoke and clay, apple and ash,
thick as the slush our feet plume

near dank knuckles of water roots, mosquito eggs,
crane feathers trembling in shadows of bass.
Toads thrash the shore and plop into duckweed.
When we dive, the water sings away
the stories of our bodies,

our throats opened: grandmother's evening dress
drifts into the dark; grandfather opens his arms
in exaltation or dismay, all of us sinking below
circling gar and algal blooms
to where horse bones

shift in the slow pull, to the rich mud we take up
and eat, our mouths ripening
like white fire.

STEVE YATES

Remember Home Art

(Old woman looking at sun swath on her carpet)

Sitting in this half-cold
room (the sun on her back
and hair, sun spilling

down to the floor,
onto the gray carpet)
her warm shadow

is real, is always
like a girl she was,
neither broken nor bent,

but dark, beckoning,
and at home
with what she is.

Window at the Med School

A long car enters the sallow lot.
Chrome and white fold the sputtering amperes
from looming street lamps. The car's white
and salmonoid lines make your window matter.
When the Lincoln stops, door seals kiss open.
The man who steps out holds a leather case,
and in this, you imagine, in a sealed bag,
is a ferret sloshing in formaldehyde, a bottle
with four hundred ephedrine, a diagram
of cellular reciprocity in mitosis.
The ferret grins as yellow as the lit asphalt.
The man's hair shines like glass. His eyes
are dark seeds. He sees you, pauses.
He has placed you in your window.

JIANQING ZHENG

Dusk at Ocean Springs, Mississippi

A man casts his net
off a weather-worn pier:
a parachute splash.

Seagulls float on wind
or beat wings, their sound
chalk-scratching.

A boy and girl appear
on the beach and kiss
into a silhouette

against sunset.
Night drifting in
like a thread of gossamer,

the man collects his net
and leaves, whistling
I Believe I Can Fly.

Up in the blue-black sky,
a new moon hangs
like a ballet slipper.

Night Swim

Perhaps tired of
sitting on the deck
watching the new moon

drifting on the pale white
of the small pond and
hearing frogs croaking

against the quiet night,
the man stands up and
plops into water

to startle the moon
into a flutter of wings,
but it rocks away

like an origami boat.
Then he flails the water
intending to turn it over;

it slithers away
like a silverfish. After
his moonplay

the man rolls over
to backstroke and
float like a log

on the moonlit ripples
sparkling like fish-scales.
He dog-paddles to shore

and sees the moon
shine like a paper lantern
above a weeping willow.

Fishing

Once the cork bobs in water
I jerk and reel the line in—
a carp fluttering into my hand,

its scales tinged with bronzy green
and its eyeballs rolling indifference.
I take the hook off its upper jaw

and dispatch it back home;
it swims toward the dense green.
Again I lift the rod over shoulder

to cast the fly, laughing at
the idea of hooking the rising moon.
Now red clouds have faded into

an expanse of purple lupines
on flanks of the mountainous sky
and night is absorbing outward

like Chinese inkwash. An instant leap
of a silver arc in the pond.
Is that the sound of moonrise?

I put up the fishing tackle
and drive, empty-handed, into the dark
rushing toward me like moths.

A Farewell to Legs

My legs became medals
by treading on a land mine
in the Vietnam jungle.

Lying alone in the sickroom,
I seemed a harp seal
rotting on the beach.

One morning a nurse came in
like a dolphin
arcing out of water

and gave me a shot; the jab
charged me up
like sunset's last radiance.

"A kiss by a wasp," I wagged,
winking at her small hands.
She chucked me under the chin,

her eyes wide at mine. I chortled,
"You choosing a melon?"
"Yes!" She blinked.

Trying to keep her stay longer,
I picked out words
like a tuner on a keyboard,

"I—feel—itchy—on—my—scars."
She stroked my leg stumps,
her fingers roaming like my soul.

To amputate her focus,
I babbled about my plan
to write *A Farewell to Legs.*

"That's great!"
She seemed to cheer,
then brushed toward the door—

the dolphin leaped back
to sea, the wink she tossed at me
splashed kerplunk.

THE POETS

LESLIE ADAMS is a recent graduate of Mississippi State University, where she earned her Master's Degree in English and served as a poetry editor for *The Jabberwock Review,* was awarded both the Eugene Butler Creative Writing Scholarship and the Albert Camus Creative Writing Scholarship, and received second place in the Southern Literary Festival Poetry Contest. She recently participated in the SonEdna Foundation Writer's Showcase, which promotes the arts in the Mississippi Delta through featured readings. Leslie is currently employed as a lecturer at Mississippi State University.

ANGELA BALL's prize winning and frequently anthologized poems and translations have appeared in journals including *The New Yorker, Atlantic Monthly, Colorado Review, Denver Quarterly, Field, Partisan Review, Ploughshares, Poetry,* and *The Southern Review.* Her books of poetry include *Kneeling Between Parked Cars* (Owl Creek Press, 1990); *Possession* (Red Hen, 1995);*Quartet* (Carnegie Mellon, 1995); and *The Museum of the Revolution* (Carnegie Mellon, 1999). Her newest collection, *Night Clerk At the Hotel of Both Worlds* (University of Pittsburgh Press, 2007), received both the Mississippi Institute of Arts and Letters Award in Poetry and the Donald Hall Prize from the Association of Writers and Writing Programs. The recipient of an Individual Writer's Grant from the National Endowment for the Arts, Ball has been a writer in residence at the University of Richmond and at Chateau Lavigny near Lausanne, Switzerland.

STEVEN BARTHELME has published fiction, non-fiction and poetry in many magazines and journals including the *The New Yorker, Atlantic Monthly, Yale Review, Epoch, New York Times Magazine, Washington Post, Texas Observer,* and others. A book of essays and occasional pieces is forthcoming from Red Hen Press in Los Angeles. He teaches at the University of Southern Mississippi.

MICHAEL BASSETT holds an M.F.A. from Vermont College and a Ph.D. from The University of Southern Mississippi. His poetry has appeared in many journals and anthologies, including *Barrow Street, Rhino, Southern Quarterly, Cider Press Review, Fugue, Lullwater Review, Concho River Review* and *Kakalak.* Pudding House Press published his chapbook, *Karma Puppets,* in 2003. His latest volume, *Waiting for Love to Make My Phone Explode,* is available from March Street Press. Winner of the 2005 Fugue Poetry Contest judged by Tony Hoagland and the Joan Johnson Award, Michael currently teaches, writes and creates visual art in south Florida.

D.C. BERRY's publications include *Vietnam Cemetery, Divorce Boxing, Zen Cancer Saloon* (chapbook), and *Vietnam Ecclesiastes*, with *Hamlet Off Stage* recently released by Texas Review Press and *A Week on the Chunky and Chickasawhay* to appear this fall from TRP. Berry, who taught thirty years in the Center for Writers, USM, Hattiesburg, divides his time between Oxford, MS, and Coons Mill, MS. At USM he won three Excellence-in-Teaching awards and was a Charles Moorman Distinguished Professor in the Humanities.

TONY BLAND is a retired counselor and itinerant Zen teacher living in rural Mississippi (Webster County). Over the past twenty years he has occasionally written poetry. His work has been published in the literary journals *Nightsun,* and *Xavier Review,* and in *The Maple Leaf Rag,* an anthology of poems read at the Maple Leaf Bar in New Orleans. In addition he has self-published *Two In Two Years,* a chapbook of poems about his parents.

RICHARD BOADA is currently a Ph.D. candidate in Poetry at the University of Southern Mississippi Center for Writers. His work has appeared or is forthcoming in *The Louisville Review, Poetry East, Limestone, Jabberwock Review, Northridge Review, Touchstone, New Madrid* and *Santa Clara Review* among others.

LOUIS E. BOURGEOIS is an instructor of English at the University of Mississippi. His most recent collection of poems, *Olga,* was published in October 2005 by WordTech Communications. His poem "A Voice in the City" was selected by Heather McHugh for inclusion in *The Best American Poetry 2007.* His newest works are *The Gar Diaries* (nonfiction) and *The Animal* (prose poems).

DEVON BRENNER is associate professor of reading and language arts at Mississippi State University. A transplanted Michigander, she's lived in Starkville, Mississippi, for ten years, where she likes watching the hummingbirds tussle at the feeder. She is the mother of Ruby, who sings, and Vaughan, who plays the drums, but she has no rhythm and cannot carry a tune. She's had one poem published, in *Hard Row to Hoe,* and has pieces forthcoming in *Inkwell.*

JACK BUTLER was born in 1944 in Alligator, in the Mississippi Delta, where his father was a Southern Baptist minister. He received undergraduate degrees in mathematics and English and an M.F.A. in Creative Writing from the University of Arkansas. He has worked as a Southern Baptist minister, fried-pie salesman, poet-in-residence, actuarial analyst, depreciation specialist, Assistant Dean of Hendrix College, and Director of Creative Writing at the College of Santa Fe.

He has published eight books—two volumes of poetry, one of short fiction, a food book, and four novels—in sixteen editions worldwide, including the Japanese-language publication of his fourth novel. He has appeared in *The New Yorker, Poetry, Poetry Northwest, The Atlantic Monthly, The New York Times Book Review, The Los Angeles Times Book Review,* the *New Orleans Review,* and many other journals

FRED CLARKE was born in 1982 and has lived in various states across the country. He currently has a B.A. in Political Science from The University of Southern Mississippi and is working on an M.A. in English. He has lived in Mississippi for the four years that he pursued his B.A. and returned to the state a year ago to prepare himself for graduate programs in creative writing.

BETH COUTURE is a Ph.D. student in fiction at the University of Southern Mississippi's Center for Writers, where she is at work on a book of short stories and a novella in prose poems. Her work has appeared in *The Georgetown Review, The Sea Oats Review,* and *Red Heart, Black Heart: The 2009 Writer's Digest Valentine's Day Collection,* and will appear in the novel *A Language of Now,* forthcoming from Chiasmus Press, and the anthology *Thirty Under Thirty,* forthcoming from Starcherone Press.

JACK CROCKER was born and raised in the Mississippi Delta. A collection of poems, *The Last Resort,* was published in 2009 by the Texas Review Press. He has published in a variety of journals (*Mississippi Review, Texas Review, Southern Poetry Review*) and is included in several anthologies: *Texas Stories and Poems; Mississippi Writers: A Reflection of Childhood; Texas Poetry Anthology.* Crocker is also a songwriter and at one time had a recording contract with Fretone Records in Memphis.

GEORGE DREW was born in Mississippi and raised there and in New York State, where he currently lives. He is the author of two collections of poetry, most recently *The Horse's Name Was Physics,* from Turning Point Press; a third, *The Hand that Rounded Peter's Dome,* will be released by Turning Point in 2010. Drew has published widely in such journals as *Antioch Review, Atlanta Review, The Baltimore Review, Beloit Poetry Journal, Cutthroat, Louisiana Literature, Mississippi Review, New Millennium Writings, North American Review, Salmagundi,* and *The Sow's Ear Poetry Review.* He is the winner of the 2003 Paumanok Poetry Award, the 2007 Stephen Dunn Poetry Award, the 2007 *Baltimore Review* Prize, and the 2008 *South Carolina Review* Poetry Prize.

KENDALL DUNKELBERG was born and raised in Iowa and moved to Mississippi fourteen years ago to teach. He lives with his wife and son in Columbus, where he is Director of Creative Writing at Mississippi University for Women, where he also directs the Eudora Welty Writers' Symposium. He has published in *The Literary Review, Osiris, Texas Review, Birmingham Poetry Review, Tar River Poetry, Poetry Southeast, Big Muddy, Valley Voices*, and *New Southerner*, and he has published a volume of poems, *Landscapes and Architectures*, and one of translations, *Hercules, Richelieu, and Nostradamus* by the Flemish poet, Paul Snoek. His second volume of poems, *Time Capsules,* will be published this year by Texas Review Press.

DEJA EARLEY's poems and essays have previously appeared or are forthcoming in journals like *Arts and Letters, Borderlands,* and *Lilliput Review.* She has received honors in several writing contests, including the 2008 Joan Johnson Award in poetry, the 2004-2005 Parley A. and Ruth J. Christensen Award, and an Honorable Mention from the Academy of American Poets in both 2003 and 2004. She recently completed a Ph.D. in English and Creative Writing at the University of Southern Mississippi and moved to the Boston area to teach at Framingham State College.

SEAN ENNIS is a Philadelphia, PA native and now lives in Water Valley, MS. He received his M.F.A. from the University of Mississippi, where he teaches creative writing and literature. He is also an instructor for the Gotham Writers' Workshop. His work has appeared or is forthcoming in *Tin House, The Greensboro Review, The Texas Review, Crazy Horse, The Mississippi Review*, and *The Best New American Voices* anthology.

BETH ANN FENNELLY's third book of poems, *Unmentionables,* was published by W. W. Norton in spring 2008. She is an Associate Professor at the University of Mississippi, and lives in Oxford, MS.

ANN FISHER-WIRTH's third book of poems, *Carta Marina*, appeared from Wings Press in 2009. She is the author of *Blue Window* (Archer Books, 2003) and *Five Terraces* (Wind Publications, 2005) and of two chapbooks—*The Trinket Poems* (Wind, 2003) and *Walking Wu Wei's Scroll* (online, *Drunken Boat*, 2005). With Laura-Gray Street she is co-editing *Earth's Body*, an international anthology of ecopoetry in English. Her awards include a *Malahat Review* Long Poem Prize, the Rita Dove Poetry Award, a Poetry Award from the Mississippi Institute of Arts and Letters, two Poetry Fellowships from the Mississippi Arts Commission, seven Pushcart nominations, and a Pushcart Special Mention. She has had Fulbrights to Switzerland and Sweden. She teaches at the University of Mississippi.

A native and long-time resident of Mississippi, JOHN FREEMAN now lives in Harvey, Louisiana, where he is a retired teacher. His poetry has appeared in *Arkansas Review*, *Hawaii Pacific Review*, *The MacGuffin*, *Roanoke Review*, and *Xavier Review*. He has published three books of poetry, the most recent *In the Place of Singing* (Louisiana Literature Press, 2005). He taught English and creative writing at Tarleton State University and Mississippi State University. He is currently poetry editor of *The Magnolia Quarterly*.

DAVID GALEF is a professor of English at Montclair State University and a co-founder of the M.F.A. program in creative writing at the University of Mississippi. He has published fifteen books, including the novels *Flesh* and *Turning Japanese* and the poetry books *Flaws* and *Lists*.

M.L. HENDRICKS studied writing at Johns Hopkins and The University of Southern Mississippi. She has published in a number of journals, including *Alaska Quarterly Review*, *Puerto del Sol* and *The New Orleans Review*. She is a 2005 recipient of the Mississippi Arts Commission Artist's Fellowship in prose.

JOHN OLIVER HODGES is a native Floridian now living in Oxford, MS, where he attends the graduate program in creative writing at Ole Miss. His poems have appeared in *Rattle*, *nth position*, *Frigg Magazine*, *Thieves Jargon*, *Mad Swirl*, *Unlikely Stories*, and *Zygote In My Coffee*. His short stories have appeared in *American Short Fiction*, *The Chattahoochee Review*, *Iron Horse Literary Review* and many other journals.

MELISSA HOLM recently completed an M.F.A. in poetry at The University of Mississippi in Oxford, Mississippi where she lived for three years. She has been published in *The American Poetry Journal*, *Plainsongs* and *The DMQ Review*. Melissa now lives in Atlanta, GA where she is the editorial assistant for *The Correspondence of Samuel Beckett Project* at Emory University.

JAMES CLINTON HOWELL is an M.A. student in poetry at the University of Southern Mississippi, and was recently an editor for the online poetry journal *Town Creek Poetry*. He manages DELTAHEAD Translation Group and writes freelance for major videogame industry publications. His poetry has appeared in *Product*.

T.R. HUMMER is Professor of Creative Writing at Arizona State University; author of ten books of poetry and prose, most recently *The Infinity Sessions: Poems* (LSU Press). He is former editor in chief of *The Kenyon Review*, *The New England Review*, and *The Georgia Review*. He has received the Hanes Poetry Prize, the Richard Wright Award for Literary Excellence, a Guggenheim Fellowship in poetry, a National Endowment for the Arts Fellowship in poetry, and three Pushcart Prizes.

JULIA JOHNSON's poems have appeared in such journals as *Third Coast, Poetry International, Cake Train,* and *The Greensboro Review.* Her first book of poems, *Naming the Afternoon,* was published by the Louisiana State University Press in 2002. She was the winner of the Fellowship of Southern Writers' New Writing Award. A native of New Orleans, she teaches in the Center for Writers at The University of Southern Mississippi in Hattiesburg.

LARRY JOHNSON was born in Natchez, MS, in 1945. He attended Mississippi College and the University of Arkansas, where he received the M.A. and M.F.A. degrees in 1970. He has published in many different magazines, including *Poetry Northwest, The Texas Quarterly, New Orleans Review,* and *The Iowa Review,* and was represented in the poetry volume of *Mississippi Writers: Reflections of Childhood and Youth* (University Press of Mississippi, 1988). *Veins,* his first book of poems, will be published in 2009 by WordTech Editions. He lives in Raleigh, NC, and teaches at Louisburg College.

SWEP LOVITT is from Mississippi and earned an M.S. in Modern European history from the University of Southern Mississippi. Lovitt spent thirty years as a coordinator for a major truckline. Publications include 60 poems in 35 mags/lit journals—*Texas Review, Poem, Mississippi Review, Visions International*—and a volume, *A Boy's Face with Swan Wings,* UKA Press, 2004.

MIRANDA MERKLEIN is a water person meandering the Gulf Coast. Her work has appeared or is forthcoming in *Oxford American, Big Muddy, The Columbia Review,* and others. She is a Ph.D. candidate in creative writing at the University of Southern Mississippi in Hattiesburg and the editor and publisher of *Journal of Truth and Consequence,* a magazine for the arts.

DAN MORRIS grew up in Issaquah, WA, 16 miles east of Seattle. He is currently a Ph.D. student at the Center for Writers at the University of Southern Mississippi. His work has recently been published in *Town Creek Poetry, Clark Street Review, Red Rock Review, Homestead Review, StringTown, Redactions: Poetry and Poetics, LitRag,* and *Xavier Review,* among others. His chapbook, *Following the Day,* was published by Pudding House, March 2007.

DARLIN' NEAL's story collection, *Rattlesnakes and the Moon*, was a 2008 finalist for the New Rivers Press MVP award and a 2007 finalist for the GS Sharat Chandra Prize. In the last two years, her work has been nominated seven times for the Pushcart Prize and appears in *The Southern Review, Shenandoah, Puerto del Sol* and numerous other magazines. Her work has been selected for the forthcoming anthologies, *Best of the Web 2009* and *Online Writing: The Best of The First Ten Years*. She is assistant professor of creative writing in the University of Central Florida's M.F.A. program.

T.A. NOONAN's first full-length poetry collection, *The Bone Folders*, won Cracked Slab Books' 2007 Heartland Poetry Prize. Her work has appeared in many journals, including *RHINO, Phoebe, specs, Harpur Palate, Foursquare*, and *88: A Journal of Contemporary American Poetry*. She is the founding editor of Flaming Giblet Press and the online journal *grain short/grain long*. In 2009 she will complete a Ph.D. in Literature and Creative Writing from the University of Southern Mississippi's Center for Writers.

CATHERINE PIERCE's poetry collection *Famous Last Words* won the 2007 Saturnalia Books Poetry Prize and was published in 2008. She is also the author of a chapbook, *Animals of Habit* (Kent State 2004). Her poems have appeared *Slate, Ploughshares, Indiana Review, Blackbird*, the anthology *Best New Poets 2007*, and elsewhere. Pierce lives in Starkville, MS, where she is an assistant professor of English and creative writing at Mississippi State University.

ALEX RICHARDSON earned a Ph.D. from the Center for Writers at the University of Southern Mississippi in 2000. His first collection of poems, *Porch Night on Walnut Street,* was published in 2007 by Plainview Press in Austin, TX. He is chair of the English Department at Limestone College in South Carolina where he teaches Creative Writing, Film History, Modern Poetry and Shakespeare. He has been awarded as a Fulbright Scholar and will spend part of 2009 teaching at the University of Madeira in Portugal.

PAUL RUFFIN, 2009 Texas State Poet Laureate, is Texas State University System Regents' Professor and Distinguished Professor of English at Sam Houston State University, where he directs the Creative Writing Program and Texas Review Press and edits *The Texas Review.* Ruffin has published two novels, three collections of stories, three books of essays, and seven collections of poetry and edited or co-edited eleven other books. He has published poetry and fiction in journals such as *Alaska Quarterly Review, Poetry, Paris Review, Prairie Schooner, New England Review, Michigan Quarterly Review,* and *Southern Review.*

JORDAN SANDERSON grew up in Hattiesburg, MS. He earned a Ph.D. from the Center for Writers at the University of Southern Mississippi, where he won the Joan Johnson Award for Poetry. His work has appeared in journals such as *Mad Hatter's Review*, *DMQ Review*, and *Double Room*, and his chapbook, *The Last Hedonist*, was published by Pudding House Publications in 2006. Jordan currently teaches at Auburn University.

DANIELLE SELLERS is originally from Key West, FL. She has an M.A. from The Writing Seminars at Johns Hopkins University. Her poems have appeared or are forthcoming from *River Styx, The Cimarron Review, Poet Lore, Poetry Southeast*, and others. She won *The Madison Review*'s 2006 Phyllis Smart Young Prize and has been a semi-finalist for the "Discovery"/*The Nation* prize. Sellers was recently nominated for the 2008 *Best New Poets* Anthology. She is currently a John and Renée Grisham Poetry Fellow in the M.F.A. program at Ole Miss where she serves as senior editor of *The Yalobusha Review*.

JEAN-MARK SENS lives in Thibodaux, LA, where he is Collection Development Librarian at Nicholls State University and teaches culinary classes at the Chef John Folse Culinary Institute as adjunct Chef. Born in France and educated in Paris, Sens has lived and taught in the American South for over fifteen years. He earned a MLIS from U.S.C. and holds degrees in English from the University of Southern Mississippi and Paris VII University, as well as an Associate in Science in Culinary Arts from Johnson & Wales. Red Hen Press in California published his first collection *Appetite* in the Fall 2004.

JES SIMMONS has lived in Natchez, Clinton, and Jackson, and is a second-generation poet whose work has appeared in *Mississippi Arts & Letters, Magnolia State Quarterly Review, College English, River City Review*, and *The James Dickey Newsletter*, among others, as well as in the anthology *Mississippi Writers: Reflections of Childhood and Youth*. Jes' late father Edgar Simmons was a noteworthy native-Mississippi poet (*Driving to Biloxi*, 1968, was a finalist for the National Book Award) and Mississippi College English professor whose students included Barry Hannah, Jack Butler, John Freeman, and Larry Johnson.

ERIN ELIZABETH SMITH is the author of the book *The Fear of Being Found* (Three Candles Press 2008) and is currently a Ph.D. candidate at the Center for Writers at the University of Southern Mississippi. Her poetry and nonfiction has previously appeared or is forthcoming in *The Florida Review, Third Coast, Crab Orchard, Natural Bridge, West Branch, The Pinch, Rhino*, and *Willow Springs* among others. Smith is also the managing editor of *Stirring* and the *Best of the Net* anthology.

YVONNE TOMEK is a full-time Instructor of English at Delta State University in Cleveland, MS, where she also teaches French grammar and literature. She has lived in Cleveland, MS, for many years with her husband, James Tomek, who also teaches English and French at Delta State. Tomek has published poetry in such journals as *POMPA, Northwoods Journal, Mississippi Valley Voices, Mississippi Today, The Birmingham Review, Dan River Anthology, Dead or Alive Poets Society, 100 Words,* and *In Other Words*. Last year her book of poetry, *A SECOND SEASON: Poems in Two Languages* was published by Northwoods Press in Thomaston, Maine.

NATASHA TRETHEWEY won the 2007 Pulitzer Prize for poetry for *Native Guard,* her 2006 collection about black Union soldiers who guarded a fort off the coast of Mississippi during the U.S. Civil War. Tretheway was born in Mississippi but grew up with her mom in Decatur, Georgia, with visits to her grandmother in Gulfport and her father, the poet Eric Trethewey, in New Orleans. She graduated from the University of Georgia (1989), where she was a football cheerleader, then went on to earn graduate degrees from Virginia's Hollins University (1991) and the University of Massachusetts at Amherst (1995). Trethewey's poems about cultural memory and ethnic identity have been winning prizes since she published her first collection, *Domestic Work,* in 2000. A National Endowment for the Arts grant allowed her to work on her 2002 collection, *Bellocq's Ophelia,* and in 2003 she received a Guggenheim Fellowship. A longtime teacher of creative writing, Trethewey is the Phillis Wheatley Distinguished Professor at Emory University.

JOHN MICHAEL TUCKER grew up in Jackson, Mississippi, where he still lives. He studied fiction writing and poetry writing at the University of Southern Mississippi. One of his short stories was a national collegiate winner for short fiction and was published in the *Allegheny Review.* His poetry has been published in the *Emerald Coast Review.*

LINDSAY MARIANNA WALKER is a Ph.D. student in English at the University of Southern Mississippi. She has served as poetry editor for the literary journal, *Juked,* since 2005. Her poetry has appeared, or is forthcoming, in *West Branch, Gulf Stream, The Southern Quarterly, The Jabberwock Review, The Bare Root Review, Voix du Vieux, Stirring,* and *Product.* She has published fiction in *Pindeldyboz* and *971 Menu,* and her play "Boy Marries Hill" appears in Gary Garrison's playwriting guide book, *A More Perfect Ten,* from Focus Publishing. Walker was recently a finalist for the Walt Whitman Award.

GORDON WEAVER taught literature and writing at colleges and universities in New York, Ohio, Colorado, Mississippi, and Oklahoma. Author of four novels, ten story collections, and a poetry chapbook, recognition of his work includes two NEA fellowships, the O. Henry First Prize, the St. Lawrence Award for Fiction, and numerous other awards and honors. He has presented more than a hundred and fifty invited lectures, readings, and workshops across the United States and overseas. Father of three, grandfather of five, he lives in Cedarburg, Wisconsin.

GREG WEISS is a Ph.D. student in poetry at the University of Southern Mississippi. His work has appeared or is forthcoming in *The Columbia Review*, *The South Carolina Review*, *The Oklahoma Review*, *The Margie Review*, and *Rattle*.

NICK WHITE graduated from Delta State University with a bachelor's degree in English and is currently finishing up his Masters degree in English from Mississippi State University. At Mississippi State, he was awarded the Eugene Butler Creative Writing Scholarship, the Albert Camus Creative Writing Scholarship for fiction, and the Howell H. Gwin Scholarship. Last year, his short story "Kin" was nominated for the *The Best American Voices* anthology. His poems are forthcoming in *The Pinch* and *Permafrost*, and he now serves as associate editor of the *Jabberwock Review*.

BRANDON WICKS received his M.F.A. from George Mason University in 2005. His work has most recently appeared in *The South Carolina Review* and in *The New Encyclopedia of Southern Culture: Volume 9: Literature*. Currently, he teaches at Emory University in Atlanta, GA, where he is at work on his second novel, "Pony Paradise."

GARY CHARLES WILKENS is currently pursuing his Ph.D. at The Center for Writers at the University of Southern Mississippi. He was the winner of the 2006 Texas Review Breakthrough Poetry Prize for his first book, *The Red Light Was My Mind*. His is a co-founder and poetry editor of *The Externalist*, and his poems have appeared in *Dicey Brown*, *The Texas Review*, *The Prague Revue*, *The Yellow Medicine Review*, *The Cortland Review*, *The Adirondack Review* and *MiPOesias*, among others.

Though he spent two years teaching in the public schools of the Mississippi Delta, JOE WILKINS now lives in Forest City, Iowa, where he directs the creative writing program at Waldorf College. His poems, essays, and stories have recently appeared in the *Georgia Review*, the *Missouri Review*, the *Southern Review*, *Pleiades*, *Tar River Poetry*, and *Slate*. His work has won an Emerging Writers Award from *Boulevard*

Magazine and the *High Desert Journal*'s Obsidian Prize for writing about the American West. He is also the 2008 recipient of the Ellen Meloy Fund for Desert Writers for his proposal to travel, observe, and write about the high plains along the eastern front of the Rocky Mountains.

CLAUDE WILKINSON's poems have appeared in numerous journals and anthologies. His first poetry collection, *Reading the Earth,* won the Naomi Long Madgett Poetry Award. In 2000, Wilkinson became the first poet to be chosen as the John and Renee Grisham Visiting Southern Writer in Residence at the University of Mississippi. He also received the Whiting Writer's Award. His book, *Joy in the Morning,* was nominated for a Pulitzer Prize in 2005. In addition to poetry, he has published literary criticism on such diverse writers as Chinua Achebe, Italo Calvino, and John Cheever. Also a visual artist, his paintings have been featured in exhibitions at the African American Museum, Carnegie Center for Arts and History, Meridian Museum of Art, Paterson Museum, and Porter Troupe Gallery, among many other invitational, juried, and solo shows.

JOHNNY WINK is a professor of English and Latin at Ouachita Baptist University in Arkadelphia, Arkansas.Wink has published one volume of poems (*Haunting The Winerunner*, August House Press) and a number of poems in magazines and journals including *The Christian Science Monitor, The Plains Poetry Journal, Christianity and Literature, The Kansas Quarterly, The Kentucky Poetry Review, and Mississippi Arts & Letters.*

WILLIAM WRIGHT earned a Ph.D. in 2009 from the University of Southern Mississippi's Center for Writers. He is author of *Dark Orchard*, published by Texas Review Press in 2005 and winner of the Breakthrough Poetry Prize for that year, as well as a recent chapbook, *The Ghost Narratives* (Finishing Line Press). Wright is founder of *Town Creek Poetry* (www.towncreekpoetry.com) and co-editor of the *Southern Poetry Anthology*. Recent work is published or forthcoming in *North American Review, Beloit Poetry Journal, New South, New Orleans Review, Tar River Poetry, Nimrod, Indiana Review, Colorado Review, AGNI,* and *Smartish Pace.*

STEVE YATES is the winner of two fellowships from the Mississippi Arts Commission for his fiction. He has published poems in *Tampa Review, The Texas Review, Folio, Borderlands: Texas Poetry Review,* and elsewhere. He has stories forthcoming in *TriQuarterly,* and published in recent issues of *Valley Voices, Harrington Gay Men's Literary Quarterly,* and elsewhere. He lives in Flowood, MS, and is Marketing Director at University Press of Mississippi.

JIANQING ZHENG, who received his Ph.D. from the Center
for Writers at the University of Southern Mississippi, has lived in
Mississippi since 1991. He is professor and chair of the Department
of English at Mississippi Valley State University where he edits *Valley
Voices: A Literary Review*. He has published a few hundred poems in
journals, including *Mississippi Review, Georgetown Review, Hanging Loose,
Poet Lore, Poetry East, Rattle, Southern Poetry Review, The Antigonish Review,*
and *The Literati*. His chapbook, *The Landscape of Mind*, won the 2001
Slapering Hol Poetry Competition. He was also a recipient of the
2004 Literary Fellowship for Poetry and a writer-in-residence for the
All-Write Project from the Mississippi Arts Commission.